ENDING DISCRIMINATION
IN SPECIAL EDUCATION

ABOUT THE AUTHOR

Herbert Grossman has worked in special education as classroom teacher, clinical psychologist, and teacher trainer. He has been a member of the faculty of fourteen universities in the United States and abroad in the departments of special education, psychology, and psychiatry. And, he has guest-lectured at more than one hundred universities. Doctor Grossman has taught and consulted in Latin America, Africa, and Europe under the auspices of such organizations as UNESCO, the Fulbright Commission, Project Hope, and the International Foundation for Education and Self Help. He directed the multicultural and bilingual special education programs at San Jose State University for sixteen years. This is his sixth book about special education.

ENDING DISCRIMINATION IN SPECIAL EDUCATION

By

HERBERT GROSSMAN, PH.D.

San Jose State University
San Jose, California

CHARLES C THOMAS • PUBLISHER, LTD.
Springfield • Illinois • U.S.A.

Published and Distributed Throughout the World by
CHARLES C THOMAS • PUBLISHER, LTD.
2600 South First Street
Springfield, Illinois 62794-9265

©*1998 by* CHARLES C THOMAS • PUBLISHER, LTD.
ISBN 0-398-06824-0

Library of Congress Catalog Card Number: 97-29378

*With THOMAS BOOKS careful attention is given to all details of manufac-
turing and design. It is the Publisher's desire to present books that are satisfacto-
ry as to their physical qualities and artistic possibilities and appropriate for their
particular use. THOMAS BOOKS will be true to those laws of quality that
assure a good name and good will.*

Printed in the United States of America
MS-R-3

Library of Congress Cataloging in Publication Data

Grossman, Herbert, 1934-
    Ending discrimination in special education / by Herbert Grossman.
        p. cm.
    Includes bibliographical references.
    ISBN 0-398-06824-0 (pbk.)
    1. Special education–Social aspects–United States.
    2. Discrimination in education–United States. 3. Minorities-Education–United States. 4.
    Educational equalization–United States. I. Title
    LC3981.G757   1997
    371.9'04–DC21   97-29378
                                                                                    CIP

To Sheena

PREFACE

There are huge disparities in the school experiences and educational outcomes of the students in our special education system. For example, students without disabilities who are poor, non-European Americans, or immigrants continue to be misplaced in special education programs. Numerous students with disabilities who are limited English proficient, migrants, or homeless are denied the special education they merit. And, gifted and talented students from these backgrounds are especially likely to be deprived of the special education services they require.

Students with disabilities and gifts and talents from these backgrounds who are correctly placed in special education often receive services that are culturally inappropriate and ill-suited to the socioeconomic, geographic, and other factors that shape the context of their lives. Students with disabilities who are limited English proficient or speak a nonstandard English dialect often experience an additional problem—linguistically inappropriate services.

The primary causes of these problems is the discriminatory practices that pervade our special education system. One of the main reasons why this discrimination exists is that special education is not special for all students. In recent years, most special educators have been attempting to individualize their pedagogy to the disabilities, gifts, and talents of their students. Psychologists have been preparing reports that suggest how they may do so, and administrators have been attempting to provide them with the tools they need to accomplish this goal. However, the assessment, instruction, classroom management, and counseling approaches that are currently being employed are inappropriate for the many poor, non-European American, immigrant, refugee, migrant, rural, and limited English proficient students in our special education programs because they are designed for European American, middle-and upper-class, English proficient students.

Prejudice, usually unconscious, toward these students is a second major source of discrimination. While some teachers may not be biased, most are. The referral and placement process is just one example of the many ways educators', psychologists', and school administrators' treatment of poor and certain non-European students reflects the biases that exist in the larger society. When teachers refer students for evaluation for possible placement in special education programs, they are more likely to refer poor and non-European American students for placement in programs for students with disabilities and less likely to refer them to programs for the gifted and talented. When special educators and psychologists evaluate these students they tend to judge their work, performance, intellectual abilities, and social skills to be lower than objective data would indicate. When selecting the most appropriate placement for students with the same behavioral and academic problems they are more likely to choose a special education program for non-European Americans and poor students and a regular education program for middle-class European American students. And, when they choose a special education program for students, they are likely to recommend a more restrictive, custodial environment for non-European Americans and poor students than for middle-class European American students.

Ending Discrimination in Special Education explains the forces that create and maintain these and other discriminatory assessment, instructional, classroom management, and counseling approaches and describes what we can do to eliminate them. The ideas, suggestions, and conclusions expressed in the book are controversial. However, I believe that it is important to tell the truth. I do not want to add my voice to those calling for half-hearted changes in our special education approaches. I want to lay out the problems and their solutions as I see them and as research dictates.

I have written *Ending Discrimination in Special Education* with two groups of readers in mind. One group is the special educators, administrators, and psychologists currently working in special education. This book is well-suited to the needs of these in service personnel. The second group are special educators, administrators, and psychologists in training and regular education teachers in training who need to acquire the competencies necessary to succeed with *all* of the students with disabilities, gifts, and talents who will be included in their classrooms. To reach this second audience, I have designed the book so that it can be used as a supplementary text in the introductory special education course offered to preservice special educators, and in the mainstreaming/full inclusion course taken by regular education teachers in-training.

ACKNOWLEDGMENTS

I would like to thank my friends and colleagues, Professors Janette Klinger and Mary Franklin for the many suggestions they made for modifying the first draft of the manuscript. As usual, my wife, who is a trained special educator, read every word of every draft of the manuscript and made invaluable recommendations for their improvement.

CONTENTS

ENDING DISCRIMINATION IN SPECIAL EDUCATION

Chapter 1

THE PROBLEM

In the 1960s and 1970s, a few special educators warned that special education was disserving students who were poor, African American, Hispanic American, or Native American. Their voices were largely ignored. In the 1980s, researchers made us aware of the many specific ways non-European American, limited English proficient, poor, immigrant and refugee, migrant, rural and other students were poorly served by special education. The effects of this information were minimal. Today, the voices are more strident and there are more of them. However, they still have little influence. In the 1990s, students with disabilities are still not able to behave, learn, and be assessed in ways commensurate with their diverse ethnic, socioeconomic, contextual, and linguistic backgrounds.

The enormous disparities between the school experiences and educational outcomes of poor, non-European American, immigrant, refugee, rural, and limited English proficient students with disabilities, and their European American middle and upper-class peers testifies to the fact that they still do not receive their just share of the special education pie or fair treatment in the special education system. They are still misrepresented—over and underenrolled—in special education programs. Those who are misplaced in special education are denied the kind of education they would profit from in regular education programs. Those who are inappropriately kept in the regular education system are deprived of the special education services their disabilities require. Students who are correctly placed in special education often receive services that are culturally inappropriate and ill-suited to the socioeconomic, geographic, and other factors that shape the context of their lives. And, students who are limited English proficient or speak

3

a nonstandard English dialect often experience a third problem—linguistically inappropriate services.

Although some school districts have cleaned up their acts, poor and non-European American students, especially those who are African Americans, Hispanic Americans, Native Americans immigrants, refugees, or migrants have been and are still grossly misrepresented in those special education programs in which placement decisions are subject to assessment bias (e.g., programs for students with learning disabilities, behavior disorders, mild developmental disabilities, gifts and talents, and so on versus those for students with physical or sensory disabilities) (1-19). While, the type of misrepresentation they experience differs from state to state and from school district to school district, in general African American, Native American and poor students are still underrepresented in programs for the gifted and talented and overrepresented in special education classes for students with behavior disorders, learning disabilities, serious emotional problems, communication disorders, and mild developmental disabilities.

Overall, Hispanic Americans and Native Americans tend to be over-represented in programs for students with learning disabilities and underrepresented in programs for the gifted and talented, but again this varies from school district to school district. Asian American students tend to be underrepresented in programs for students with learning disabilities, serious emotional problems, and behavior disorders and overrepresented in programs for students with speech disorders. In fact, in some school districts as many as 50 percent of the Asian American students receiving special education services are in such programs.

African Americans experience the greatest overrepresentation in programs for students with disabilities. Although they account for only 12 percent of the elementary and secondary school population, they constitute 28 percent of the total enrollment in special education. And, they are especially overrepresented in programs for students with mild developmental disabilities and behavior disorders.

Non-European American students who are also limited English proficient are even more likely to be misrepresented in special education programs. A number of new bilingual special education programs for limited English proficient gifted and talented students have been initiated in recent years. However, on a nationwide basis these students have and continue to be underrepresented in such programs because there are so few bilingual special educators (20-23).

To some educators, underrepresentation of limited English proficient students in programs for students with behavior disorders, emotional problems, learning disabilities and mild developmental disabilities is an improvement because it signifies that fewer of them are being misplaced in programs for students with disabilities. However, the truth is that many poor immigrant and refugee students need these kinds of special education services because of the extreme physical and psychological deprivation they experienced before they emigrated to the United States. Limited English proficient students with disabilities who remain in bilingual regular education programs are instructed by teachers who are not prepared to provide them with the special education services they require.

While researchers have studied the effectiveness of the special education services provided to students with disabilities and gifted and talented students, very few of them have been interested in studying whether these services are equally effective with poor and middle and upper-class students, European American and non-European American students, and English proficient and limited English proficient students. The limited evidence available suggests that most, but not all, of the very few programs specifically designed to deliver cultural, contextually, and linguistically appropriate services to non-European American or limited English proficient students with disabilities or gifted and talented are effective, at least to some degree (24-32). However, the majority of special education programs are not designed with the needs of poor, non-European American, and limited English proficient students in mind (33-42). Studies of these programs indicate that with very few exceptions, African American, Hispanic American, Native American, and poor students earn lower grades and score lower on standardized tests than their European American middle-class peers. They are also less likely to be returned to mainstream classes, to graduate from high school, to continue their studies after high school, to achieve vocational success, to be employed, or to earn a good living.

Poor students are especially likely to do badly in special education regardless of their ethnic background. For example, a national study found that when students with disabilities were divided into four groups based on their socioeconomic status, their dropout rates were: lowest quartile—26.7 percent, second quartile—25.0 percent, third quartile—17.2 percent, highest quartile—6.7 percent. Thus, the dropout rate for students in the two lowest socioeconomic-class groups was almost four times as great as that of students in the highest group (32).

The number of poor and non-European American students with disabilities that will suffer these injustices in the future is on the rise (43-47). Immigrant and refugee children continue to enter our country in very large numbers. By the year 2000, because of immigration and unequal birth rates in the United States, non-European Americans are expected to comprise one-third of the U. S. population. Between 1979 and 1989 the numbers of Hispanic American, European American, and African American children living in poverty increased by 29, 25, and 6 percent respectively, leading to an overall increase of 19 percent. If we do not correct the inequality in the special education system even more students will suffer the consequences of our failure to do so.

We know the specific ways non-European American, limited English proficient, poor, immigrant and refugee, migrant, rural and other students are poorly served by special education. However, we cannot provide poor, non-European American, immigrant, refugee, rural, and limited English proficient students with disabilities with appropriate educational services, unless we first understand why the special educational system is structured in an unjust manner and why special educators, administrators and psychologists continue to treat so many students unfairly. It's time to investigate the motives and rationales of the individuals who continue to disserve them and what can be done to change things.

REFERENCES

These references include evidence regarding ethnic and socioeconomic-class differences in student enrollment in special education.

1. Artiles, A. J., & Trent, S. C. (1994). Overrepresentation of minority students in special education: A continuing debate. *Journal of Special Education, 27*, 410-437.
2. Benavides, A. (1988). *High Risk Predictors and Prereferral Screening for Language Minority Students*. Revised. ERIC ED 298 702.
3. Bowman, J. E. (1988). *A Study of Special Education Referral and Placement Practices in Montgomery County Public Schools* (Maryland). ERIC ED 301 004.
4. Chinn, P. C., & Hughes, S. (1987). Representation of minority students in special education classes. *Remedial and Special Education, 8* (4), 41-46.

5. Florey, J., Tafoya, N. (1988). *Identifying Gifted and Talented American Indian Students: An Overview.* ERIC ED 296 810.

6. Harry, B. (1994). *The Disproportionate Representation of Minority Students in Special Education: Theories and Recommendations.* Alexandria, VA: National Association of State Directors of Special Education.

7. MacMillan, D. L. (1988). *"New" EMR's. Chapter One.* ERIC ED 304 829.

8. Murphy, J., & Simon, R. (1987). *Minorities Issues in Special Education: A Portrait of the Future. News Digest#9.* Washington, DC: National Information Center for Handicapped Children and Youth.

9. National Information Center for Children and Youth with Handicaps. (1988). *Minority Issues in Special Education: A Portrait of the Future.* Washington, DC.

10. Ochoa, A. M., Pacheco, R., & Omark, D. R. (1988). Addressing the learning disability needs of limited-English proficient students: Beyond the language and race issues. *Learning Disabilities Quarterly,* 11, 257-264.,

11. Office of Civil Rights. (1987). *Elementary and Secondary School Civil Rights Survey, 1986.* National Summaries. ERIC ED 304 485

12. Plata, M., & Chinn, P. C. (1989). Students with handicaps who have cultural and language differences. In R. Gaylord-Ross (Ed.), *Integration Strategies for Students with Handicaps.* Baltimore: Brookes.

13. Ramirez, B. (1990). Federal policy and the education of American Indian exceptional children and youth: Current status and future directions. In M. J. Johnson & B. Ramirez (Eds.), *American Indian Exceptional Children and Youth. Report of a Symposium.* ERIC ED 322 706.

14. Ramirez, B. A., & Johnson, M. J. (1988). *American Indian Exceptional Children: Improved Practices and Policy.* ERIC ED 298 713.

15. Reschly, D. J. (1988). Minority MMNR overrepresentation and special education reform. *Exceptional Children,* 54 (4), 316-323.

16. Ryan, M. B. (1988). *Assessing Limited English Proficient Students for Special Education.* ERIC ED 316 045.

17. Schwenn, J. O. Hamon, G. T., & Jones, J. R. (1989). *Research on Service Patterns for Exceptional Children in the Rural Southeast.* ERIC ED 316 989.

18. Serwatka, T. S., Deering, S., & Stoddard, A. (1989). Correlates of the underrepresentation of Black students in classes for gifted students. *Journal of Negro Education,* 58 (4), 520-530.

19. Yancey, E. (1990). *Increasing Minority Participation in Gifted Programs.* ERIC ED 324 393.

The references below indicate that limited English proficient students with certain disabilities are under represented in certain special education programs.

20. Bergin, V. (1980). Special Education Needs in Bilingual Programs. Rosslyn, VA: National Clearinghouse for Bilingual Education.

21. Nuttall, E. V., Landurand, P. M., & Goldman, P. (1983). A Study of Mainstreamed Limited English Proficient Handicapped Students in Bilingual Education. ERIC ED 246 583.

22. Ortiz, A. A., & Yates, J. R. (1981). Exceptional Hispanics: Implications for

Special Education Services and Manpower Planning. A report of the Texas Education Agency, Council for Personnel Preparation of the Handicapped, Task Force on Exceptional Hispanics. Austin: University of Texas

23. Vasquez-Chairez, M. (1988). Bilingual and Special Education: Procedural Manual for Program Administrators. Crosscultural Special Education Series, Vol. 1. Sacramento: California State Department of Education.

These references provide evidence that programs designed to deliver cultural, contextually, and linguistically appropriate services to non European American or limited English proficient students with disabilities or gifted and talented are effective, at least to some degree.

24. Berney, T. D., & Cantalupo, D. (1990). Bilingual Education Talented Academy: Gifted and Talented, Project BETA, 1988-1989. Evaluation Section Report and Executive Summary. OREA Report. ERIC ED 322 679.

25. Berney, T. D., & Hriskos, C. (1990). Great Opportunities for Optional Resources to Improve the Talents of Gifted Bilingual High School Students: Project GO-FOR-IT 1988-1989 OREA Report. ERIC ED 321-539.

26. Berney, T. D., & Keyes, J. (1998). Computer Writing Skills for Limited English Proficient Students project. (COMPUGRAPHIA. LEP). 1987-1988. ERIC ED 311 719.

27. Berney, T. D., & Velasquez, C. (1990). Project COMPUOCC. LEP Evaluation Section Report and Executive Summary. OREA Report. ERIC ED 322 678. Applied Developmental Psychology. Norwood, NJ: Ablex.

28. Foster, C. G. (1986). Special education program for Native American exceptional students and regular program staff. Rural Special Education Quarterly. 8 (3), 40-43.

29. Lichtenstein, S. J. (1987). A Study of Selected Post-School Employment Patterns of Handicapped and Nonhandicapped Graduates and Dropouts. Unpublished doctoral dissertation, Urbana-Champaign, IL: University of Illinois, Urbana-Champaign.

30. Miller, R. C., Berney, T. D., Mulkey, L., & Saggese, R. (1988). Chapter 1/P.S.E.N. Remedial Reading and Mathematics Program 1986-1987. Final Evaluation Report and Evaluation Summary. OREA Evaluation Report. ERIC ED 302 049.

31. O'Connor, S. C., & Spreen, O. (1988). The relationship between parents socioeconomic status and education level, and adult occupational and educational achievement of children with learning disabilities. Journal of Learning Disabilities, 21 (3), 148-153.

32. Owings, J., & Stocking, C. (1986). High School and Beyond, a National Longitudinal Study for the 1980's. Characteristics of High School Students Who Identify Themselves as Handicapped. ERIC ED 260 546.

These references provide evidence that non European American and poor students who attend programs that are not designed to provide them with culturally, contextually, and linguistically appropriate special education services do poorly.

33. Asch, A. (1984). The experience of disability: A challenge for psychology. American Psychologist, 39 (5), 529-536.

34. Blackorby, J., & Kortering, L. J. (1991). A third of our youth? A look at the problem of high school dropout among students with mild handicaps. Journal of Special Education, 25 (1), 102-113.

35. Bruck, M. (1985). The adult functioning of children with specific learning dis abilities: A follow-up study. In I. Siegel (Ed.), Advances in Applied Developmental Psychology. Norwood, NJ: Ablex.

36. Cardoza, D., & Rueda, R. S. (1986). Educational and occupational outcomes of Hispanic learning-disabled high school students. Journal of Special Education, 20 (1), 111-126.

37. Harnisch, D. L., Lichtenstein, S. J., & Langford, J. B. (1989). Digest on Youth in Transition Volume 1. ERIC ED 279 118.

38. Individuals with Disabilities Education Act (20 U. S. C., Sections 1400-1485; Education of the Handicapped Act Amendments of 1990).

39. Palmateer, R. (1988). Educare: Evaluation of a Transition Program for Culturally Disadvantaged and Educationally Handicapped Youth. Executive Summary. ERIC ED 3405 791.

40. Weissman, C. S., Archer, P., Liebert, D. E., Shaw, E., & Schilley, D. (1984). The Impact of Early Intervention and Other Factors on Mainstreaming. Final Report, 3/1/83-4/30/84. ERIC ED 245 033.

41. Welsh, W., & Schroedel, J. (1982). Predictors of Success for Deaf Graduates of the Rochester Institute of Technology. (Paper Series #46). Rochester, NY: Department of Planning and Evaluation Systems, National Technical Institute for the Deaf.

42. Wyche, L. G., Sr. (1989). The Tenth Annual Report to Congress: Taking a significant step in the right direction. Exceptional Children, 56 (1), 14-16.

These references discuss population trends.

43. Bureau of the Census. (1988b. Money, Income and Poverty Status in the United States: (Advance Data from the March 1989 Current Population Survey). Current Population Reports, Series P-60, No. 166, U. S. Department of Commerce, Washington, D.C.: U. S. Government Printing Office.

44. Hodgkinson, H. L. (1992). A Demographic Look at Tomorrow. ERIC ED 359 087.

45. National Information Center for Children and Youth with Handicaps. (1988). Minority Issues in Special Education: A Portrait of the Future. Washington, D.C.

46. Puente, T. (1991). Latino child poverty ranks swell. Hispanic Link Weekly Report, 9 (35), 1,2,8.

47. Wald, J. (1996). Culturally and Linguistically Diverse Populations in Special Education: A Demographic Analysis. Reston, VA: Council for Exceptional Children.

Chapter 2

PREJUDICE AND DISCRIMINATION

One of the main, if not the main cause of inequality in special education is prejudice. Prejudice and discrimination toward people who are different than we are are pandemic diseases of human kind. Witness the tension, conflicts and sometimes even outright wars caused by religious differences in Northern Ireland, and India; by ethnic differences in Iraq, the former Yugoslavia, the Philippines, China, the former Soviet Union, Rwanda, and Burundi; socioeconomic-class in Great Britain; by skin color differences in South Africa, Australia, Great Britain, and Mexico; by language differences in Canada, India and by whether individuals are immigrants or native born citizens in Germany and other Western European countries just to name a few.

Let's look at the way such prejudice affects the educational programs of two countries in more detail (1-4). In Sweden, a country thought by many to be a model of egalitarianism, limited Swedish speaking students are submerged in regular classes taught in Swedish even though they do not understand Swedish and are given only two or three hours a week of instruction in their native languages. Cultural characteristics that are different than those expected in the schools are not accepted. No provision is made to adapt the curriculum of such courses as family life and sex education to the beliefs and values of immigrant and other minority groups. Children cannot be excused from attending such courses even when their content goes against the children's cultural or religious beliefs. Swedish working class students are also treated in a prejudicial manner by their teachers. For example, working class children tend to be placed in tracks for "low achievers" even if their levels of achievement are on a par with those of their more affluent classmates who are placed in higher level tracks.

Educational inequality in Great Britain is similar to what we experience at home. In general, working-class students do not achieve at the same level as middle and upper-class students. With the exception of students from Indian and East African backgrounds, immigrant and refugee students and the native born children of immigrants and refugees from Pakistan, Bangladesh, Turkish Cyprus, and the Caribbean Islands do less well than British children from European backgrounds.

As in our country, there is considerable prejudice against certain groups. In some areas, prejudiced white students who are in the majority make it difficult for students of color to learn because they are so anxious about the treatment they receive from their white peers. Many teachers believe that different ethnic groups have different intellectual capacities and that black children, especially, inherited lower intellectual ability.

When pupils are assigned to bands (tracks) for their secondary schooling on the basis of test scores, teachers are far more likely to refer students from Afro-Caribbean backgrounds to a band lower than that predicted by their test scores. Teachers are also more likely to assign students from Afro-Caribbean backgrounds to CSE examination tracks (an examination which does not make students eligible for university studies) rather then "O" level examination tracks (an examination which makes students eligible for university studies) even when their test scores indicate that they should be studying for O level examinations. A law passed in 1988 requiring that the daily worship in public schools must be mainly Christian is an affront to Muslim, Jewish, and other non-Christian students.

There is also a great deal of prejudice against non-English language speaking students. Teachers tend to view students who come to school speaking their native language rather than English as deficient, not different. Rather than placing students in bilingual education programs where they can gradually shift from their native language to English as the language of instruction, students are submerged in classes where they cannot understand their teachers.

These kinds of prejudices may help to explain why nonwhite immigrant students are often assigned to lower streams/bands (tracks) and to schools that are "educationally subnormal," why there is an over-representation of migrant and minority children in special education programs, and why, as in our country, students from Afro-Caribbean backgrounds are overrepresented in programs for the behaviorally disordered.

A law passed in 1988 that gives parents the right to select the schools their children attend has led to an increase in school segregation by color, because many white parents have withdrawn students out of ethnically mixed schools. And, many Afro-Caribbean parents have withdrawn their children from racist public schools and enrolled them in all black schools run by religious organizations. As a result, some public schools are 85- 98 percent non-white British and some church schools have established quotas limiting the percent of non-white students they will accept.

Special education in the other Western European countries that belong to the Organization for Economic Cooperation and Development is as biased as it is in our country (5). "Minority pupils" especially bilingual and Muslim students are overrepresented in special education because the educational systems use special education as an alternate placement for students who need bilingual education or who lack access to an appropriate education. In Eastern Europe countries, it is the Romani (Gypsy) children who are misplaced in special education.

"Gypsy children from the first grades were automatically stuck into special schools for the mentally handicapped. They weren't retarded, but they were handicapped: they didn't speak the language, and the deficiency had become a widespread excuse for segregation and indeed incarceration" (6, p. 163).

It seems that we humans have an inborn potential to reject and mistreat people who are different than we are. We don't have to reject and mistreat them, but we have the latent capacity to do so. There is no reason to assume that Americans, who are members of the human race, should have escaped this universal potentiality to reject and mistreat people who are different than we are. The evidence consistently indicates that we have not. And that includes our special education system as well.

My first experience with prejudice in special education occurred when I was teaching in a residential treatment center for emotionally disturbed and delinquent adolescents. Somewhere around ninety to 95 percent of the students were European Americans; less than ten percent were African Americans or Hispanic Americans. Whenever, and it wasn't very often, a white female would pair off with a black male, the staff would discuss the diagnostic implications of her behavior. For most of my colleagues, there were only two possible reasons for her behavior. Either she was rebelling against society by breaking a sacred taboo or she felt too inferior to believe that she could attract a white male. Very few staff members could conceive of the possibility that she just liked him.

I do not think things have changed very much since then. Ask yourself these three questions. What assumptions would a group of European American teachers make about the reasons why an African American high school student would hang out with a group of European American students? Now ask yourself what assumptions they would make about the reasons why a European American male student would hang out with a group of African American male high school students. Finally, ask yourself what they would think about a European American female student who hung out with a group of African American male students.

In 1964, I was fortunate to be given the chance to start an experimental day treatment school for inner city adolescents who were incarcerated and awaiting placement in correctional facilities, residential treatment centers, or mental hospitals. The director of the agency who gave me the opportunity was a visionary. He retired two years later and was replaced by someone with a more traditional approach.

After I had been running the program for almost three years, the new director and the chief psychiatrist of the agency came to have a look at what we were doing. They read the students records, observed the classes, and interviewed the teachers and therapists. A couple of weeks later, they said that they wanted me to return six students to the courts. They were too dangerous to be allowed to remain in the community, I was told. And, if they caused trouble in the community, the agency and the program would be held responsible.

But they were all doing well, I protested. None of them had gotten into trouble and they all had been in the program for at least a year. My protests had no affect. The agency still wanted me to get rid of the six students. I refused. First they insisted, then they threatened, then they fired me and returned the students to the court themselves. The students were all African Americans or Hispanic Americans. Not a European American among them.

I have often thought about what those kids must have felt when they were punished even though they had been behaving well, getting better, and overcoming their problems. I also thought a great deal about why the chief psychiatrist and the director of the agency treated them so unjustly. I came to the conclusion that neither of them came to the school to look for African American and Hispanic American kids to ship back to court. I have no reason to believe that they hated African Americans or Hispanic Americans. I believe that they didn't know anything about non European American kids. And not understanding them they were afraid of them. They probably were trying to protect society and the agency's good name but they picked the wrong kids to protect them from. There is no doubt in my mind, that if those kids had been European Americans they would have had a better shake from society and its agents.

There is also little doubt in my mind that the same thing would easily happen today. As we will see below, students of color with disabilities are still more likely to be placed in more restrictive custodial settings than European American students.

All the students that attended the experimental day treatment school were evaluated by a court or agency psychologist. The results of their evaluations were a lesson in biased assessment. All but one of the Hispanic American and African American students had IQ scores that would have qualified them for a program for the developmentally disabled (mentally retarded). All of the European American students had normal or higher IQ scores. As you might expect, none of the so-called retarded students were actually retarded. If they had been retarded, they would not have been able to outsmart us so often.

Times have not changed very much. African Americans, Hispanic Americans, Native Americans, and other students of color are still assessed with biased instruments. And, they are still misplaced in programs for the developmentally disabled and denied access to programs for students with gifts and talents.

I would like to describe just one more incident that illustrates another kind of prejudice that affects the lives of the students we are trying to help. When I was working as a psychologist in a school for pregnant teenagers in the Southeast Bronx, one of the students, a 15 year-old dark skinned Puerto Rican American, Lucila, and her 17 year-old sister, Josephina, were shoplifting and stealing tips customers had left for the waiters and waitresses in restaurants. They claimed they needed the money to support themselves. But they would stop, they assured me, if they had a legal way to get the money they needed.

They lived with their mother, an alcoholic, who survived on welfare. Lucila had attended classes irregularly during the previous year until she transferred to our special school. She had sixth grade reading skills and fifth grade math skills. She seldom did any homework or even came to class prepared, claiming that she was too tired to concentrate on school work. However, she maintained that she wanted to complete high school so she could get a good job and support her child. She said that she had stopped her occasional use of marijuana and various pills, (she had never used cocaine or heroine), when she learned that drugs could harm her baby.

Josephina was in her senior year. She had done moderately well in school. However, she had begun to skip school regularly a couple of months before I had met her. She told me that although she had hoped to graduate and attend college, she had given up on the idea because she could not imagine how she would be able to support herself and go to school at the same time. Josephina denied using any drugs except marijuana, and then only occasionally.

Thinking that the girls might change their behavior once they could afford to do so, I met with the family caseworker in the welfare department and asked if the department could provide them with the additional money they claimed they needed to tread the straight and narrow path. Their caseworker answered, "You don't know these people. They'll waste the money on drugs. The only work people like them can do is cleaning houses and taking care of kids." When I asked who she meant by people like them, she didn't answer. However, I felt she meant "Negroes," or Puerto Ricans. A few days later I met with her supervisor. I made it a point to mention that I was a clinical psychologist and faculty member of the department of psychiatry of Albert Einstein Medical School. I also stated my belief that the case worker was prejudiced and unwilling to help the girls. The result of the meeting was that the supervisor agreed to increase the family's benefits and to provide financial support to Josephina through a vocational rehabilitation program if she became a full time college student.

To make a long story short, Josephina started attending school regularly, graduated from high school and enrolled in college. The last I heard, she was doing well.

Lucila began to attend our school more regularly and claimed that she had stopped her delinquent behavior. She had her baby during the summer after I had started a new assignment at Albert Einstein. I dropped by the school a while later to check on my ex-clients. I found out that she was addicted to heroine. When I visited her and her new boyfriend I found them living in a filthy hovel. There was no food in the house for them or the infant. (Lucila was not breast-feeding.) I felt I had no choice but to refer them to child protective services.

Lucila had almost nothing going for her. She had little education and less ambition. Her survival skills were too inadequate to meet the challenges of teenage motherhood. Poverty and hopelessness had taken their toll. She had given up and allowed heroine to take over her life. Josephina had a lot more going for her. With a little help she was able to see a light at the end of the tunnel, which was all she needed to get back on track.

Lucila and Josephina had been pushed so far down that they needed considerably more than society was willing to invest in them until they entered the very expensive criminal justice system. Unfortunately, this attitude still prevails today.

Most educators believe that they are not biased against non-European American and poor students. The average American would probably like to believe that too. But they are wrong! While some teachers may not be biased, most are. The facts are depressing, but they are true and need to be faced. Teachers', psychologists', and school administrators' treatment of poor and certain non-European students reflects the biases that exist in the larger society.

Teachers expectations of their students tend to be prejudicial (7-13). Many special educators and special education students expect the European American middle-class students in their classes to do better academically than non-European American and poor students beginning in preschool and continuing through their college careers. And, they expect European American middle-class students to be more intelligent, even when students' achievement test scores, grades, and school histories would predict otherwise. In experiments in which educators are given the exact same information about students except for their ethnic or socioeconomic backgrounds, they attribute higher academic and intellectual potential to European American students than African American students and Hispanic students. They have the same prejudicial expectations for middle-class students in comparison to poor students. Educators also expect many non-European American students, especially African Americans, to be more disruptive and deviant than European Americans.

Since we often think we see what we expect to see, these biased teacher expectations become self-fulfilling prophesies. As a result, these biases contribute to the lack of African American and Hispanic American students in programs for the gifted and talented and their overrepresentation in programs for students with behavior disorders.

Teachers tend to evaluate non-European American students' behavior in a biased manner (12, 14-21). When teachers evaluate the severity or deviancy of students' behavior problems, they judge the exact same transgressions as more severe or deviant when they are committed by African American male students than when they are committed by European American students. African American students who are seen as fun-loving, happy, cooperative, energetic and ambitious by African American teachers are viewed as talkative, lazy, fun-loving, high-strung, and frivolous by their European American teachers. This too contributes to the lack of African American and Hispanic

American students in programs for the gifted and their overrepresentation in programs for students with behavior disorders.

When teachers and school psychologists refer students to special education programs, evaluate them for possible placement in special education programs or select the most appropriate placement for them, their evaluations of non-European Americans and poor students are biased (12, 22-34). Teachers are more likely to refer poor and non-European American students for evaluation for possible placement in programs for students with disabilities and less likely to refer them to programs for the gifted and talented. When evaluating them, they tend to judge their work, performance, intellectual abilities, and social skills to be lower than objective data would indicate.

When selecting the most appropriate placement for students with the same behavioral and academic problems, educators and psychologists are more likely to choose a special education program for non-European Americans and poor students and a regular education program for middle class European American students. When they choose a special education program for students, they are likely to select a program for students with mild developmental disabilities for non European Americans and poor students and a learning disabilities program for middle-class European American students. They also are likely to recommend a more restrictive, custodial environment for non-European Americans and poor students than for middle-class European American students.

Being poor and African American places students at even greater risk to be on the receiving end of teacher bias. For example, teachers are 3.5 times more likely to identify poor African American students as retarded (developmentally disabled) than their European American peers. Teachers are also more likely to refer poor African American students to programs for students with disabilities and less likely to refer them to programs for the gifted and talented.

"Professionals in education may view cultural differences among black students as indicators of deficiencies. This perception can lead to a student being identified as being below normal or abnormal on measures of adaptive behavior and social development. Scoring low or scoring as abnormal on these measures can in turn lead to placement in classrooms for emotionally disturbed and educable mentally retarded pupils" (12, p. 21).

There is also evidence that teachers evaluate Asian Pacific Island

American students in a biased manner. There appear to be three reasons for this. First, believing that all of them are good students, they fail to notice their academic problems and neglect to refer students with learning disabilities for special education evaluation. Secondly, Asian American students tend to internalize their emotional problems rather than act them out. Even though they may be experiencing serious emotional problems, their suffering is less obvious and less disruptive than that of students who act out their problems. As a result, they are less likely to be noticed by teachers or to be referred for special education services. Third, because teachers welcome the quiet unobtrusive behavior of many Asian Pacific Island Americans, they often fail to recognize when it may be a sign of problems.

Most, but not all, studies indicate that teachers tend to treat non-European American and poor students unfairly (35-47). In comparison to European American students, teachers praise African Americans less and criticize them more. The praise they give them is more likely to be routine, rather than feedback for a particular achievement or behavior. And when teachers praise them for a specific behavior, it is more likely to be qualified ("your work is almost good enough to be put on the board") or in the case of females, more likely to be for good behavior than for academic work.

Teachers interact more with European American students than with African Americans, especially males, and give them less attention. In comparison to European American students, educators are less likely to respond to African American male students' questions or to direct questions to them. Unlike the preferential treatment many teachers give their brightest European American students, they give bright African American students, especially females, the least attention and criticize them the most. While European American teachers typically demonstrate considerable concern and interest in European American females' academic work, they pay less attention to African American female students' academic work than to their social behavior. Teachers encourage European American female students in intellectual and academic areas, while they encourage and praise African American females in areas involving social skills.

Educators tend to use different classroom management techniques with African American and European American students. In general, teachers of classes with high percentages of African American students are more likely to be authoritarian and less likely to use an open classroom approach. Teachers spend more time on the look-out for possible misbehavior by African American students, especially males. When male students misbehave, educators are prone to criticize African American males' behavior and to use more severe punishments including corporal punishment and suspension with them. And when females misbehave, teachers treat African Americans more harshly than European Americans.

Teachers also relate to Hispanic students in a discriminatory manner. Although Hispanic students tend to prefer more positive reinforcement and feedback from their teachers than most European American students, teachers praise them less often and give them less positive feedback when they answer correctly or perform well. Teachers are also less likely to encourage them when they need encouragement, to accept their ideas, and to direct questions to them.

Poor students also receive unfair treatment in school. Beginning in primary school, teachers give them less attention and fewer rewards. Educators provide poor students, especially males, fewer social and instructional contacts, but more disciplinary and control contacts. And, when they discipline students, teachers in schools that serve predominantly poor students are more likely to endorse or use corporal punishments, verbal punishments, or suspension than teachers in schools attended by middle-class students.

Prejudice and discrimination against non-European American and poor students is still rampant. Although not all teachers and psychologists are biased, it is clear that teachers' and psychologists' bias against non-European American and poor students contributes to their overrepresentation in special education programs for students with behavior disorders, emotionally disturbances, and mild developmental disabilities; their underrepresentation in programs for the gifted and talented; and their lack of success in special education. Non-European American and poor students will continue to be misrepresented in special education programs and not receive the kind of special educational services they deserve until educators behave more democratically and serve the needs of the population as a whole. Thus, the elimination of teacher prejudice and discrimination is the first and most important step special educators can take to ensure that only students who require special education services are referred to and accepted into special education programs and that once accepted, they receive appropriate special education services.

Lamentably, we have not made a great deal of progress in this area. When I ask myself why teachers continue to treat students in such discriminatory ways, I find three explanations. First, I believe that prejudice and discrimination are part of the human condition. We seemed to be programmed to discriminate against people who do not belong to our group, or who look, talk, think, or act differently from us. Prejudice and discrimination are an ever-present danger against which we constantly must be vigilant.

Secondly, much of our prejudice is unconscious (48-50). Wanting to see ourselves in a good light, we hide our prejudice from ourselves. Sometimes, we purposely do not notice that we call on one group of students more than another, expect more from one group than another, or reward and punish one group more than another. At other times, we allow ourselves to become aware of the different ways we treat different groups of students, but justify and rationalize our inappropriate behavior. We do this by attributing characteristics such as linguistic inadequacy, aggressiveness, cultural inferiority, laziness, and other prejudicial stereotypes that pervade our society to the students we discriminate against, thereby convincing ourselves that these characteristics justify the manner in which we treat them. Being unaware of the discriminatory way we treat students and/ or justifying it, we have no need to change our behavior.

Finally, many teachers discriminate against students who are unlike them because they fear them. This is clearly true of the many European American teachers who keep African American students at a distance, avoid calling on them, remain on the lookout for signs that they are about to misbehave and cause trouble, use strict and severe forms of discipline with them, and so on. In general, people fear the unknown. In addition, European American teachers are aware of the ways in which African Americans, Hispanic Americans, Native Americans, and poor people in general were and continue to be treated by our society. They know about the unemployment, poverty, racism, discrimination, and so on that these students and their families experience. They sense the resentment, anger, and mistrust these students harbor towards the European American establishment that treats them so unjustly. And, they are well aware of the periodic angry explosions that have rocked our society when these groups could not take any more. Is it any wonder that down deep they are afraid of how their students may react to them?

Not too long after World War II ended, a large number of Puerto Rican Americans began moving into my neighborhood. My mother and father, unlike most people in the neighborhood, were friendly with them, partly because they met the new arrivals when they bought second-hand furniture or other things in our store. But my friends and I had little if anything to do with the Puerto Rican guys.

One day, Matty and I met these two good-looking Puerto Rican girls who lived up the block. We were no more than 14 or 15 years-old, so nothing much was going to happen. We talked under one of the girls' stoops for a couple of hours and arranged to meet them after school the next day. But, when I came home from school the next day (actually I always went directly to the store to check in) my mother told me to forget my plans. When I asked what plans, she told me that one of the girl's mothers had asked her to keep me away from her daughter. I asked my mother why. Because I wasn't Puerto Rican, she explained. That puzzled me. I could understand that my mother might not want me to hang around with Puerto Rican girls (actually I knew that neither of my parents felt that way), but I couldn't believe that Puerto Rican parents would not want their daughters to hang out with me. If, at that moment, someone had told me that that meant that I was prejudiced, I would have laughed in his or her face. How could I be prejudiced, I would have argued. I liked a Puerto Rican girl.

REFERENCES

These references discuss educational inequality in Great Britain and Sweden.

1. Ekdering, L. & Kloprogge, J. (Eds.) (1989). *Different Cultures Same School: Ethnic Minority Children in Europe.* Berwyn, PA: Swets & Zeitlinger. Commission for Racial Equality(1987). Learning In Terror. London.
2. Mortimer, P., Sammons, P., Stoll, L., Lewis, D.,. & Ecob, R. (1988). *School Matters-The Junior Years.* London: Open Books.
3. Tomlinson, S. (1989). Ethnicity and educational achievement in Britain. In Ekdering, L. & Kloprogge, J. (Eds.). *Different Cultures Same School: Ethnic Minority Children in Europe.* Berwyn, PA: Swets & Zeitlinger.
4. Troyna, B. (1987). (Ed.) *Racial Inequality in Education.* London: Tavistock.

Special education inequality in Western European countries is described in this publication:

5. Organization for Economic Cooperation and Development (1987). *Immigrant Children at School.* Paris: OECD.

The misplacement of Rom children in special education is discussed in the following reference.

6. Fonseca, I. (1996). *Bury Me Standing: The Gypsies and Their Journey.* New York: Vintage Books

The references listed below describe teachers' biased expectations for students:

7. Campos F. (1983). *The Attitudes and Expectations of Student Teachers and Cooperating Teachers Toward Students in Predominantly Mexican-American Schools: A Qualitative Data Perspective.* ERIC ED 234 026.
8. Dao, M. (1991). Designing assessment procedures for educationally at-risk Southeast Asian-American students. *Journal of Learning Disabilities,* 24 (10), 594-601,629.
9. Dusek, J. B., & Joseph, G. (1983). The bases of teacher expectancies: A meta-analysis. *Journal of Educational Psychology,* 75, (3), 327-346.
10. Grant, L. (1984). Black females' "place" in desegregated classrooms. *Sociology of Education,* 57, 98-110.
11. Matute-Bianchi, M. E. (1986). Ethnic identities and patterns of school success and failure among Mexican-descent and Japanese-American students in a California high school: An ethnographic analysis. *American Journal of Education,* 95 (1), 233-255.
12. Serwata, T., Dove, T., & Hodges, W.)1986). Black students in special education: Issues and implications for community involvement. *Negro Educational Review,* 37 (1), 17-26.

13. Wilkerson, M. A. (1980). The effects of sex and ethnicity upon teachers' expectations of students. *Dissertation Abstracts International,* 41, 637-A.

The following references discuss bias in teachers' evaluations of students.

14. Elliot, S. N., & Argulewicz, E. N. (1983). The influence of student ethnicity on teachers' behavior ratings of normal and learning disabled children. *Hispanic Journal of Behavioral Sciences,* 5(3), 337-345.
15. Haller, E. J., & Davis, S. A. (1980). Does socioeconomic status bias the assignment of elementary school students to reading groups? *American Educational Research Journal,* 17 (40, 409-418.
16. Ishi-Jordan, S. (1992). *Effects of Students' Racial or Ethnic Background on Teacher Expectations and Intervention Selection for Problem Behaviors.* Paper presented at the Topical Conference on Cultural and Linguistically Diverse Exceptional Children. Minneapolis, MN.
17. Kim, Y. J. (1983). Problems in the delivery of the school-based psycho-educational services to the Asian immigrant children. *Journal of Children in Contemporary Society,* 15(3), 81-89.
18. Scheinfeld, D. R. (1983). Family relationships and school achievement among boys of lower-income urban black families. *American Journal of Orthopsychiatry,* 53 (1), 127-143.
19. Taylor, J. B. (1983). Influence of speech variety on teachers' evaluation of reading comprehension. *Journal of Educational Psychology,* 75 (5), 662-667.
20. Tobias, S., Cole, C., Zibrin, M., & Bodlakova, V. (1981). *Bias in the Referral of Children to Special Services.* ERIC ED 208 637.
21. Yao, E. L. (1987). Asian-immigrants students--Unique problems that hamper learning. *NASSP Bulletin,* 71(503), 82-88.

These references deal with teachers and psychologists' biased evaluations of students in or referred to special education.

22. Argulewicz, E. N. (1983). Effects of ethnic membership, socioeconomic status, and home language on LD. EMR, and EH placements. *Learning Disability Quarterly,* 6 (2), 195-200.
23. Argulewicz, E. N., & Sanchez, D. T. (1983). The special education evaluation process as a moderator of false positives. *Exceptional Children,* 49 (5), 452-454.
24. Bickel, W. E. (1982). Classifying mentally retarded students: A review of placement practices in special education. In K. A. Heller, W. H. Holtzman, & S. Messick (Eds.), *Placing Children in Special Education: A Strategy for Equity.* Washington, DC: National Academy Press.
25. Collier, C. (1986). *The Referral of Hispanic Children to Special Education: A Comparison of Acculturation and Education Characteristics of Referred and Nonreferred Culturally and Linguistically Different Children.* ERIC ED 271 954.
26. Fetterman, D. M. (1986). Gifted and talented education: A national test case in Peoria. *Educational Evaluation and Policy Analysis,* 8 (20, 155-166.

27. Frame, R. E., Clarizio, J. G., Porter, A. C., & Vinsonhaler, J. R. (1982). Interclinician agreement and bias in school psychologists' diagnostic and treatment recommendations for a learning disabled child. *Psychology in the Schools,* 19, 319-327.

28. Individuals with Disabilities Education Act (20 U. S. C., Sections 1400-1485; Education of the Handicapped Act Amendments of 1990).

29. Leinhardt, G., Seewald, A. M., & Zigmond, N. (1982). Sex and race differences in learning disabilities classrooms. *Journal of Educational Psychology,* 74 (6), 835-843.

30. Low, B. P., & Clement, P. W. (1982). Relationships of race, and socioeconomic status to classroom behavior, academic achievement, and referral for special education. *Journal of School Psychology,* 20 (2), 103-112.

31. Mercer, M. M. (1982). Reassessing the large number of black children in special education classes: A challenge for the 80's. *Negro Educational Review,* 33 (1), 28-33.

32. Pickholtz, H. J. (1977). *The Effects of a Child's Racial-Ethnic Label and Achievement Differences on School Psychologists' Decisions.* Unpublished doctoral dissertation, Pennsylvania State University.

34. Tobias, S., Cole, C., Zibrin, M., & Menell, C. (1982). *Special Education Referrals: Failure to Replicate Student-Teacher Ethnicity Interaction.* ERIC ED 224 221.

Bias in teacher-student interactions is the focus of the following references.

35. Bickel, F., & Qualls, R. (1981). *The Impact of School Climate on Suspension Rates in the Jefferson County Public Schools.* Paper presented at the annual meeting of the American Educational Research Association, Boston.

36. Buriel, R. (1983). Teacher-student interactions and their relationship to student achievement: A comparison of Mexican-American children. *Journal of Educational Psychology,* 75 (60, 889-897.

37. Glackman, T., Martin, R., Hyman, I., McDowell, E., Berv, V., & Spino, P. (1980). *Corporal Punishment in the Schools As It Relates to Race, Sex, Grade Level and Suspensions.* Philadelphia: Temple University, National Center for the Study of Corporal Punishment in the Schools.

38. Grant, L. (1985). Race-gender status, classroom interaction, and children's socialization in elementary school. In L. C. Wilkinson, & C. B. Marrett (Eds.), *Gender Influences in Classroom Interaction.* New York: Academic Press.

39. Grossman, H., & Grossman, S. (1994). *Gender Issues in Education.* Needham, MA: Allyn & Bacon.

40. Guilmet, G. M. (1979). Instructor reaction to verbal and nonverbal styles: An example of Navajo and Caucasian children. *Anthropology and Education Quarterly,* 10, 254-266.

41. Hamilton, S. (1983). The social side of schooling. *Elementary School Journal,* 83, 313-334

42. Moore, W. L., & Cooper, H. (1984). Correlations between teacher and student background and teacher perception of discipline problems and disciplinary techniques. *Psychology in the Schools,* 21, 386-392.

43. Richardson, R. C., & Evans, E. T. (1991). *Empowering Teachers to Eliminate Corporal Punishment in the Schools.* Paper presented at the annual conference of the National Black Child Developmental Institute. Washington, DC.

44. Simpson, A. W., & Erickson, M. T. (1983). Teachers' verbal and nonverbal communication patterns as a function of teacher race, student gender and student race. *American Educational Research Journal,* 20 (2), 183-198.

45. Stevens, L. B. (1983). *Suspension and Corporal Punishment of Students in the Cleveland Public Schools, 1981-1982.* Cleveland, OH: Office of School Monitoring and Community Relations.

46. Washington, V. (1982). Racial differences in teacher perception of first and fourth grade pupils on selected characteristics. *Journal of Negro Education,* 51, 60-72.

47. Woolridge, P., & Richman, C. (1985). Teachers' choice of punishment as a function of a student's gender, age, race and I. Q. level. *Journal of School Psychology,* 23, 19-29.

Evidence that teachers hide their prejudices from themselves while they treat students in a discriminatory manner is included in these publications.

48. Simpson, A. W., & Erickson, M. T. (1983). Teachers' verbal and nonverbal communication patterns as a function of teacher race, student gender and student race. *American Educational Research Journal,* 20 (2), 183-198.

49. Taylor, M. (1979). Race, sex and the expression of self-fulfilling prophecies in a laboratory teaching situation. *Journal of Personality and Social Psychology,* 37 (6), 897-912.

50. Feldman, R., & Donohoe, L. (1978). Nonverbal communication of affect in interracial dyads. *Journal of Educational Psychology,* 70 (6), 979-986.

Chapter 3

CULTURALLY, CONTEXTUALLY AND LINGUISTICALLY INAPPROPRIATE SPECIAL EDUCATION SERVICES

CULTURALLY INAPPROPRIATE EDUCATIONAL APPROACHES

Some governments use education as a means of cultural or ethnic domination. In the past, the colonial governments that seized most of Africa and Asia and many of the missionaries that accompanied them used education to pacify and control the population, to modify the local culture, to prepare some of the locals for specific and limited kinds of work such as clerks and lower level administrators , and so on. In South Africa under the Afrikaner regime, black South African teachers were required to follow the official curriculum in the schools in black townships and homelands. Pretending to follow a separate but equal educational policy, the amount the Afrikaner government spent on educating black South African students was only between 13 and 24 percent of what it spent on white South Africans (1-4).

Hitler attempted to eradicate the Romani (Gypsies) in concentration camps. Since then, some Eastern European countries have been trying to eradicate their culture and way of life by requiring them to attend schools especially established for them that are designed to encourage them to adopt non-Romani ways.

In Israel students from Arab and Jewish backgrounds have different school experiences. For example, Arabic and Hebrew are both official languages and students are taught in their native language. However, Hebrew is a required second language in Arab language schools but Arabic is an optional second language in Hebrew language schools. And, Hebrew is the language of instruction at the university level. Although the study of Jewish culture is part of the curriculum in Arabic language school, Arab culture is rarely included in Hebrew language schools. The government provides many more very expensive technical high schools to Israeli students from Jewish backgrounds than it makes available to Arab students, even though Jewish Israeli students are more likely to enroll in the academic rather than vocational tracks (5-8).

One does not have to spend much time in schools set up by the Indonesian government in Jakarta for Dani students in Irian Jaya and the schools in the Amazon jungle and the Andes mountains set up by the Peruvian and Ecuadorian governments and religious organizations to see that teachers expend considerable effort on encouraging and requiring students to assimilate to the dominant culture's way of life. The same would apply to Norwegian schools for Lapps, the schools set up by the ruling class in Guatemala for the descendants of the Mayans, Australian schools that enroll Aboriginal students, and to many other school systems that provide disservices not services to indigenous peoples (9,10).

Schools in the United States, like in many other countries, have historically served the needs of the majority ethnic, cultural, and power group: in our case the European American middle-class majority. Once European Americans succeeded in wresting control of the territory that presently comprises the United States from the Native Americans and Hispanic Americans who shared it with them, they installed their approach to life from the Atlantic to the Pacific, Alaska, and Hawaii.

For many years, the European American way of life, including the educational system that developed to serve the needs of the upper-class and middle-class European Americans who had the power and influence to shape it, reigned supreme with no effective challenges to it. That is not to say that other cultures did not continue to survive. However, they survived in a powerless state. Most Native Americans were confined to their reservations; African Americans were subjected to stringent restrictions—first slavery and then segregation; and the Hispanic Americans who inhabited the lands taken from Mexico were considered to be inferior and treated as second-class citizens.

Over the years many events contributed to a change in the status quo. Immigration from Mexico, Puerto Rico, and other Latin American countries, China, Japan, the Philippines, and Eastern Europe increased the numbers of persons who were not prepared for or able to adapt easily to the established educational system. Segregation was ended in most areas of American life, including education. The American working-class unionized and gained political power. Large numbers of African Americans and Hispanic Americans gained the right to vote. With all of these developments, the demand for educational reform grew louder and louder.

One of the reformers' demands was to stop insisting that non-European Americans act and function like students from the dominant culture. This demand has not been met except in isolated cases.

Their second demand was to make education culturally relevant to all students. They insisted that school personnel should be sensitized to the importance of educationally relevant ethnic and socioeconomic-class cultural differences and the special challenges and problems poor students have to deal with because of their economic situations. They wanted educators to be trained to take such differences into consideration when planning school programs and selecting instructional, classroom management, counseling, and assessment techniques for non-European American and poor students.

This demand has never been met. American schools have not adapted their educational approaches to the cultural needs of their non-European and poor students. There are some excellent culturally relevant education programs. However, by and large the American educational system provides non-European American students with culturally inappropriate instruction, classroom management, counseling, and assessment services that do not suit their educational and psychological needs. We still expect students to adopt the prevailing middle-class European American culture. As a result, many students with disabilities are offered culturally inappropriate educational services.

This is reflected in the following quotation, which summarizes the results of a national survey of the opinions of special education experts and parents of exceptional students about the state of the educational services for non-European American students with disabilities.

The current educational system has a mainstream cultural bias which adversely affects the education of students from minority backgrounds. This bias is

manifested in preconceived expectations about children from diverse cultures
that are limiting and inaccurate. In addition, lack of awareness, sensitivity and
understanding of diverse cultures by school personnel interfere with the education of students and the development of productive relationships with
parents...In general, the current instruction curricula, materials/methods and
service delivery models are inadequate for meeting the educational needs of
children from minority backgrounds...Existing methods are not adequate to
correctly assess/identify students from diverse backgrounds and determine
appropriate educational services. Therefore, there is an overrepresentation or
underrepresentation of students from minority backgrounds in various educational programs (11, p. 5-7).

The opinion of these experts is supported by a great deal of research
evidence (12-18).

The vast majority of special educators who teach in ethnically
diverse schools are not knowledgeable about their students' religious
beliefs, values, customs, life-styles, learning styles, behavior styles, and
so on. They do not know about the ways in which the economic problems of students living in poverty affect their learning. They are
unaware of the trauma many refugee students experienced prior to
arriving in the United States. They do not appreciate the difficulty
limited English proficient students experience while trying to learn in
a language they do not understand and adjust to a strange and often
frightening school environment. And, they do not think that it is
important to adapt their methods to the diverse needs of their students. For example, a recent study found that when special educators
and regular educators were asked to prioritize the skills and competencies that teachers needed in order to succeed with their students,
European American educators rated multicultural competencies less
important than regular education competencies while African
American educators rated them as more important (19).

As a result, many poor and non-European American students (especially those who are immigrants, refugees, or limited English proficient) are often exposed to assessment, instruction, classroom management, and counseling techniques that are appropriate for European
American middle-class students with disabilities, but inappropriate for
them. Having been assessed in culturally inappropriate ways, these
students may have individual education plans with goals that do not fit
their needs. Taught in teaching styles that do not match their cultur-
ally-influenced learning styles, they may progress less rapidly than

their European American peers. When they are exposed to culturally inappropriate classroom management techniques, they are less likely to change their behavior and be accepted in mainstream classes. Counseled in inappropriate ways, they can have difficulty understanding, appreciating, and accepting the knowledge and advice their teachers give them. And when their parents are exposed to similarly culturally inappropriate counseling, they are less likely to become involved in their children's education.

CONTEXTUALLY INAPPROPRIATE
EDUCATIONAL APPROACHES

The special educational approaches that predominate in most schools are ill-suited to the context or conditions of many poor and non-European American students' lives (16, 20-26). For example, immigrant and refugee students are unlikely to receive the education services they require, and therefore, likely to do poorly in school, and to be misplaced in special education programs. Too often they do not receive the assistance they require to overcome the culture shock they experience upon entering a new and strange environment. As a result, they may react angrily and aggressively towards teachers and systems they do not understand and cannot easily adjust to. Or they may become sullen, depressed, and withdrawn. These behaviors can lead educators to refer such students to be assessed for the kinds of emotional problems that require special educational services. This is especially true of students who have never attended school because they come from rural areas or internment camps and/or grew up in cultures that have no written languages. Even when their culture shock passes, they need more help than they typically receive to learn how to learn in classes taught in foreign languages and unfamiliar teaching styles. This, too, can interfere with their learning and lead them to be inappropriately placed in special education programs for the learning disabled or the retarded. Refugee students who suffer the psychological effects of the war, famine, and persecution they experienced at home or in internment camps are most likely to lack the assistance they need to overcome their problems.

Special educators who work with refugee and immigrant students need skills in instructing students with special needs and managing the special problems they bring to school. And, they need to maintain a high degree of tolerance for behavior which students cannot control while their students are adjusting to their new educational environments.

Like foreign-born students, Native American students who live on reservations live in a region separate from mainstream America where they speak a language other than English. And they, too, are ill-prepared to adjust to and profit from a curriculum typically offered in mainstream schools that encourage beliefs and values which conflict with their communities that is often taught in a language they do not understand, by teachers who are unprepared to succeed with them in schools. And like immigrant students, they are susceptible to experiencing culture shock, identity conflicts, and feelings of alienation, confusion and frustration.

Contextual problems make it difficult for poor non-European American migrant students to actualize their potential for learning. Attending school irregularly, losing considerable time traveling with their families from job to job, enrolling in numerous schools during the academic year, all contribute to their poor achievement. Lack of a stable home base, inadequate medical care, poverty, and prejudice are examples of other contextual problems that complicate their lives. In addition, while migrant students can be helped by educational programs geared to their needs, school systems that have been designed for students who are permanent members of the community often add to their problems rather than contribute to solving them.

This is no different than conditions for migrant students in many other countries. For example, at a period of great movements of populations across national borders, governments tend to be particularly miserly and prejudiced when it comes to the educational needs of the children of their immigrant, refugee, and invited workers populations. Whether we consider Pakistani in Norway; Koreans in Japan, North African Muslims in France; West Indians, Afro-Caribbeans and Pakistani in Great Britain; or Turks in Australia and Germany, immigrant children are cultural and linguistic misfits whose considerable cultural, linguistic, and educational needs are seldom met. In Germany, for example, invited workers and their children are considered and treated as temporary residents whose children are not entitled to the same educational benefits as native born Germans. In some provinces they are taught in German schools and in others they study in schools staffed by Turkish teachers recruited and supervised by the Turkish government. In Australia, Turkish students are incorporated into the public schools but they are taught almost exclusively in English in classrooms in where Anglo-Celtic values and content dominate the curriculum.

Rural students with disabilities face many contextual problems. Those from rural families that rely on seasonal activities such as fishing, agriculture, timber and so on may not be able to attend school during certain times of the year. In addition, it is difficult for school systems to provide services to small numbers of students scattered over vast land areas with major transportation problems.

The contextual problems that confront poor homeless students with disabilities are horrendous. Many do not have their basic food, clothing and shelter needs met. They have four times as many health problems and twice as many chronic diseases, but they have less access to medical care and are less able to follow the health regimes prescribed by physicians. They move from place to place and shelter to shelter and attend school erratically. They are more likely to need special education services than students who lead more stable lives. However, the transient nature of their existence makes it difficult, if not impossible, for them to either comply with school systems' insistence on receiving certain documents or to be available for long periods of time while schools implement their inflexibly slow-moving special education assessment and placement processes.

When one considers the numbers of poor urban, rural, homeless and migrant students with disabilities and the large numbers of immigrant and refugee students whose contextual needs are not met by the American educational system, it becomes clear that many students are not receiving an appropriate special education.

LINGUISTICALLY INAPPROPRIATE
EDUCATIONAL APPROACHES

In many parts of the world, governments treat problems of language diversity as a political, not an educational issue. For example, after taking control of Tibet the Chinese government quickly closed all schools run by Tibetan monks. Today there is only one elementary school in Lhasa, Tibet that is permitted to use the Tibetan language after the third grade and they receive no government funds. The Chinese government requires all other schools in Tibet to use Mandarin Chinese. This is not the case in the Cantonese-speaking areas of China. There they can use Cantonese even though Mandarin is the official language of the country. The Chinese government also requires all schools in Tibet to follow the prescribed curriculum. As a result, less than one percent of students who begin primary school stay the course (27).

Under the Afrikaner regime, black South African teachers were required to use Afrikans as the language of instruction in the schools in black townships and homeland. This was true even though 93 percent of them were in favor of using English rather than "the language of the oppressor" (1-4). In Indonesia, all students are instructed in the language and dialect that is prevalent on the island of Java which is home to the politically dominant group in the country. In Ghana, because the government wants business people and government officials to be proficient in English, it has decreed that all students must be taught in English after the third grade. As a result, children from poor and rural areas, who are extremely unlikely to ever need English, are taught in English despite the fact that they do not understand what they are being taught and most of their teachers are not proficient enough in English to use it effectively as the language of instruction. Students' inability to understand English is one of the main reasons why only one percent of students who complete the sixth grade in Ghana acquire the knowledge and skills expected of them. Thus, although it is obvious that English should not be the language of instruction for most students, a political decision has been made to sacrifice these children's educational needs for the benefit of the children of the influential elite.

In a nation such as ours that continues to be a haven for immigrants, huge numbers of students begin school without the ability to profit from instruction in English. Although estimates of how many limited English proficient students there are in the schools vary, it is probable that almost 8 million American youngsters have a non-English background either because they were born elsewhere or they grew up in the United States in a home where another language was spoken. Over 3 million of these students scored in the lowest 20 percent on tests of English proficiency. Over 5 million scored in the lower 40 percent. Whichever of these two figures one uses, it is clear that millions of students are not proficient enough in English to function in English-only classes without considerable difficulty. Experts suggest that approximately 10 percent of the student population require special education services. Using this guideline to estimate the number of LEP students who require special education yields an estimate of between 354,900 and 528,400 students with disabilities who are not proficient enough in English to function in English-only special education programs or to be assessed using English language assessment procedures (28, 29).

The appropriate instructional services required by limited English proficient students has been the subject of a number of court decisions and federal laws. In 1974, in *Lau vs. Nichols,* the Supreme Court unanimously decided that schools must provide special assistance to limited English proficient students in the form of linguistically appropriate educational services (35). In 1979, in *Dyrcia S. et al. v. Board of Education of the City of New York,* the court determined that limited English proficient students with disabilities had the same right (32). The Bilingual Education Act of 1968, Education for Handicapped Children Act of 1974 (Public Law 94-142) and the 1990 amendments to the act, Equal Educational Opportunities Act of 1972, Section 504 of the Rehabilitation Act of 1973, and the Civil Rights Act of 1964 also require school districts to provide linguistically appropriate educational services to limited English proficient students with disabilities (30, 31, 33, 34, 36).

Currently the vast majority of these students are not receiving linguistically appropriate special education services. Thus, the Education of the Handicapped Act Amendments of 1990 state that:

> Services provided to limited English proficient students often do not respond primarily to the pupil's academic needs. These trends pose special challenges for special education in the referral, assessment, and instruction services for our Nation's students from non-English language backgrounds (28).

Nowadays we know a great deal about how to educate limited English proficient students with and without disabilities (37-40). Unfortunately, the availability of bilingual special education (teaching students math, social studies, and other content areas in their native languages, while they are learning English as a second language) is restricted by the scarcity of bilingual personnel. Assuming that a bilingual special educator could serve 15 limited English proficient students and it were possible to assign students who all spoke the same language to each teacher (a very unlikely assumption) it would require between 23,000 and 35,000 bilingual special educators to serve all limited English proficient students with disabilities. Between 1979, when the federal government began to provide financial assistance to encourage universities to train bilingual special educators, and 1987, universities that prepared bilingual special educators produced only 257 graduates (41). Since 1987, there has been a decrease rather than an increase in the number of university programs in the field. Therefore it is reasonable to assume that there are probably significantly fewer than 1,000 trained bilingual special educators to fill at least 23,000 positions. In addition, except for a few programs which train special educators to work with students who speak a Native American language and one program that trains teachers to work with students who speak a Chinese or a Filipino dialect or Vietnamese, these programs all focus on Spanish-speaking students. Thus, students who speak any of the almost two hundred languages that are not included in these programs and students who live in areas that are not served by any of these programs cannot count on being taught by trained bilingual special educators.

While some school districts have bilingual special educators on their staffs, many others provide bilingual special education services by teaming a monolingual special educator with a bilingual aid who provides limited English proficient students with disabilities with the additional bilingual instruction they require to learn. However, their numbers are also limited by the lack of potential bilingual aids and the money to hire enough bilingual aids to serve limited English proficient students who speak many different languages. This is an especially difficult problem for school districts that serve a linguistically diverse population such as the Los Angeles School District which serves students who speak over one hundred different languages.

The National Coalition of Advocates for Children studied the services currently provided to limited English proficient students with disabilities (42). A child advocate stated:

If in addition to being limited in his English proficiency, that child is also handicapped, that child is really doubly handicapped because he is very unlikely to get any sort of instruction or assistance in his own language (42, p. 54).

Another advocate reported:

The Division of Special Education (and) the Board of Education have been well aware of the acute shortage of bilingual clinicians to evaluate children, and bilingual teachers to service children who have been recommended for placement in the bilingual special education program. To date, their efforts at recruitment have been almost totally unsuccessful (42, p. 57).

One of the handful of Southeast Asian school psychologists currently employed in schools in the United States reported:

Right now as a (Southeast Asian) school psychologist I have ...at least 93 referrals from the school system (42, p. 54).

A Burmese mother who wanted her daughter placed in special education described her frustrating experiences with the school system in the following words:

There was a gap of three months, March to May, when the COH (Committee on the Handicapped) did not get in touch with me...When I called them this time, I was informed that I should try and locate an individual or agency to do the evaluation in Burmese...I contacted a number of these agencies, but without any success.

Around this time, I also suggested that I might be allowed to interpret for my daughter. This suggestion they absolutely refused to entertain. It was also then that they informed me that it was incumbent upon me to find a Burmese-speaking psychologist (42, p. 55).

Some school districts are reluctant to identify limited English proficient students who may have disabilities because they are unable to provide the bilingual assessment and educational services such students would require. As a result, many limited English proficient students with disabilities are not evaluated, placed, or even referred to special education.

Because of the severe shortage of bilingual teachers and aids, a number of school districts have opted to serve their limited English proficient students with disabilities through programs that combine English as a second language and sheltered English (37, 39, 43-50). In these programs students first develop some English proficiency in an English as a second language program. Then they are taught subjects such as math, science, and social studies in a sheltered/controlled English vocabulary at their level of English comprehension while they continue to improve their English proficiency in their English as a second language class. The available evidence suggests that when this combined approach is adapted to the special needs of students with disabilities it helps them to become proficient in English (37, 39, 43-46).

Training special educators to use English as a second language and sheltered English techniques is a practical goal for special education personnel preparation programs. Unlike training in bilingual special education, it does not require a bilingual professor for each of the languages spoken by students' in their service areas. Nor does it require recruiting bilingual students. Anyone who speaks English can learn to use the techniques. Nevertheless, extremely few personnel preparation programs offer such training. Therefore, this option is not readily available to students and school districts. As Cloud has pointed out:

> Currently, a paucity of TESOL (Teachers of English to Speakers of Other Languages) programs provide crossover training in special education, and few special education programs encourage specializations in TESOL. Professionals are left to find their own training opportunities at conferences and workshops (43, p. 2).

As noted above, most limited English proficient students with disabilities are not in bilingual special education or English as a second language programs. Those that are not identified receive no special education services. Those who are placed in regular special education programs are taught in English without regard to their linguistic needs (51-53). Submerged in English without the skills necessary to profit from the instruction they receive, students are at risk for joining the ranks of students with disabilities who tune out their teachers, cut classes, and drop out of special education before graduating from high school.

The numbers of unserved or inadequately served limited English proficient students with disabilities is appalling. A study of students who, at least, were placed in special education revealed that the individual education plans of only 2 percent of limited English proficient students with disabilities included bilingual instruction in their native language and none included English as a second language instruction. The authors of the report concluded that, "The results of this study suggest that a student's bilingualism and level of English proficiency exert little influence on the IEP Committee's selection of instructional goals and objectives" (53, p. 563, 567).

The personnel shortage could be alleviated to a considerable degree if universities initiated bilingual and English as a second language special education programs. Evidently, professors still do not care enough about limited English proficient students to do so. Judging from the fact that the federal government has not renewed funds to support bilingual teacher preparation programs, it appears that our Congress persons are not terribly concerned about such students either.

School districts could assist their limited English proficient students by giving priority to bilingual teachers, aides, and psychologists when hiring new staff and by offering financial incentives for bilingual personnel. In the business world, supply and demand influences the salaries people receive. Why should that not be the case in education as well?

Unfortunately it is not. Prejudice against bilingual education and the resistance school districts face when they attempt to give priority to bilingual applicants restrict their ability to provide their limited English proficient students with bilingual special education services. Many individuals are against any use of students' native languages in the classroom. Some of them erroneously believe that providing students with bilingual education endangers the preeminence of English as the language of the United States. Others are merely ignorant of the effectiveness of bilingual education.

Sometime in the mid1980s, I was hired by a school district in California to give a week long workshop on nonbiased assessment and instruction to selected teachers, counselors, and psychologists. The school district needed to offer the workshop because it was out of compliance with California requirements that limited English proficient students with disabilities be assessed and taught in their native languages by bilingual educators and psychologists. On the first morning of the workshop, just before I met with the forty or so people who were attending, an administrator told me something that I should have known from the get-go. Almost in passing, she gave me a "by the way I think you should know that we just adopted a policy of not hiring any new special educators, counselors, or psychologists who are not Spanish speaking. And, the non-Spanish speaking staff are threatening to sue the school district."

Well, I took a deep breath, changed my lesson plan, and walked into the room. Instead of starting the workshop as I had planned, I began by asking them to discuss the new hiring policy. Almost immediately, I discovered that the bilingual staff were sitting on one side of the room and the nonbilingual staff were on the other. I had walked into the lion's den and opened up Pandora's box.

Bilingual special education works. Immersing limited English proficient students in English as quickly and as completely as possible does not work. While it takes only a year or two for students to become proficient enough in a second language to carry on every day conversations–basic interpersonal communication skills–it usually takes at least 5 years to reach the level of proficiency in a second language that is required to learn subject matter–cognitive academic learning proficiency (37, 39). If students with disabilities are instructed in subject matter in a second language too soon, they will not be able to benefit optimally from such instruction. They may lose their self-confidence, think that they are dumb, lose interest in school, and so on. On the other hand, postponing teaching students math, social studies and other content areas until students are sufficiently proficient in English would be equally disastrous.

In addition, there is considerable evidence that switching students from their native language to a new language before they have acquired cognitive academic learning proficiency can stunt their language development in either language. However, once students have acquired cognitive academic learning proficiency in one language, they are able to transfer their understanding of the logic and rules of language to the learning of a second language. Thus, students taught in their native language until they have developed "languageness," read better and achieve more in school than those who are immediately taught in a second language. This is especially important for students with learning disabilities (37, 38).

The question of what language they should be taught and assessed in is not purely an educational issue. As elsewhere, politics influence educational decisions. U. S. citizens disagree about the role of students' native languages, and they tend to fight about their differences in the political arena, not the school building. The political movement afoot to eliminate bilingual education is unjustified educationally. It reminds me of the policies of the Communist Party in China and the Afrikaners in South Africa.

Students with disabilities also come to school speaking different dialects. People disagree about how teachers should react to them (54-71). Many educators, including many special educators, believe that the English dialects spoken by many poor African American students (black English/Ebonics), the dialects spoken by Native Americans, Hispanic Americans, Hawaiian Americans (Hawaiian pigeon), and certain regional dialects spoken by poor European Americans such as the ones spoken in Appalachia (mountain English) and in the greater New York City Metropolitan Area (New Yorkese) are inferior to standard English (the English dialect used in textbooks, newspapers, television news programs, found in grammar books, and typically used by most middle and upper-class European Americans) and should be eradicated.

Experts, however, tend to consider dialect variations to be linguistic differences rather than linguistic deficiencies. Their opinion has prevailed in the federal courts. For example, in 1979, a United States District court judge ruled in favor of 15 African American students who claimed that they were denied an equal education because their school did not take their nonstandard English dialect into account. While this ruling only affected schools within the jurisdiction of the court, it has set a national tone. Judge Joiner, the presiding judge reflected the knowledge of the day in his ruling.

The court does not believe that language differences between 'black English' and standard English to be a language barrier in and of itself.

The unconscious but evident attitude of teachers toward the home language of the plaintiffs causes a psychological barrier to learning by the student... The child who comes to school using the 'black English' system of communication and who is taught that this is wrong, loses a sense of values related to mother and close friends and siblings and may rebel at efforts by his teacher to teach reading in a different language.

If a barrier exists because of the language used by the children in this case, it exists not because the teachers and students cannot understand each other, but because in the process of attempting to teach the students how to speak standard English the students are made somehow to feel inferior and are thereby turned off from the learning process (72, p. 18, 26, 36, 41-42).

Despite research findings that nonstandard English dialects are not inferior forms of English, and court opinions that teachers should not discriminate against them, many special educators continue to do so. Three discriminatory practices are especially noxious.

One of the ways in which special educators and others discriminate against nonstandard English speakers is to allow their judgments about students' work to be influenced by the dialect in which they express themselves. In general, teachers incorrectly rate the quality and accuracy of the English of speakers of standard English higher than nonstandard English. Even when students' work is identical or of equal quality, teachers judge the oral and written work of students who speak in a black English, or with a Hispanic, or a working-class accent to be poorer than students who speak standard English. And, African American students who speak black English are rated lower than those who speak more standard English (73-80).

A second way special educators and others discriminate against nonstandard English speakers is by evaluating them with instruments written in standard English. Although in the 1970s, a few studies found that nonstandard dialect speakers are not penalized when they are assessed in standard English (81-84), the vast majority of research at the time and virtually all that has been carried out since then indicates that nonstandard dialect-speaking students who are poor, African American, Native American, Hispanic American, or from Appalachian areas perform poorly when they are assessed in standard English (85-88, 90, 91, 93-96, 105-108). There is also considerable evidence that these biased results can lead educators to underestimate students' academic achievement, learning potential, and language ability and to incorrectly refer them to special education programs for nonexistent learning disabilities, developmental disabilities, and communication disorders (89, 91, 94, 95).

The following are some of the causes of dialect bias that penalize nonstandard, dialect-speaking students during the assessment process.

- Questions on assessment procedures are often asked using vocabulary that is not familiar to students (i.e., "behind the sofa" rather than "in back of the couch," "beginning to climb" instead of "starting to climb " (108). As a result students appear to lack information and skills that they actually possess and would be able to demonstrate if they understood the question or directions.

- Some dialect speakers may read material that is written in their own dialect better than material in standard English (104).

- Students tend to remember better material that is in their dialect (85, 94).

- Students are better able to discriminate between sounds that are present in their own dialect (88, 92, 102).

- Students may misunderstand items and directions because they are given in a different dialect . As an example, European American students who are asked to find which of four pictures shows "delight" may have little difficulty identifying the picture of a girl happily eating an ice cream cone. However African American students who do not speak standard English may hear de (the) light and select the picture of a boy reading who needs a light (97).

- What may appear to be articulation problems and other types of speech disorders can be omissions and substitutions that conform to speech patterns present in students' dialect (93, 106).

I believe that special educators should never assess nonstandard English dialect speakers with standard English instruments. And I tell my students that. However, realizing that not everyone will agree with me, I advise them that if they do use them with the wrong students, as a bare minimum, they should at least try to avoid these potential problems in the following ways (91, 95, 98, 99, 103, 105, 106). They should make sure students understand the directions and the items included in any assessment procedure and when necessary use alternate instructions in both dialects, and to express the contents in both dialects. They should become knowledgeable about the characteristics of the dialects spoken by the nonstandard English speakers and avoid mistaking dialect differences for possible speech disorders (87, 109, 110).

They should not consider differences in oral reading due to dialect differences such as mispronunciations, adding or omitting endings that indicate plurals tense and the like as reading errors. And they should accept answers that conforms to students' dialect as correct even though they may not be acceptable according to the manual.

A third way many special educators treat nonstandard English speakers in a discriminatory manner is by correcting their nonstandard English speech and requiring them to learn to speak standard English.

They typically offer three reasons to justify their actions.

1. *Although nonstandard English dialects are not substandard, they interfere with students' academic progress* (56, 63). The evidence regarding this contention is mixed. Most studies have found that speakers of nonstandard dialects do not have difficulty learning to read (60, 111, 113,116-118, 121, 122). "One need not speak a dialect in order to understand it." (68, p. 150)

A few researchers have reported findings that indicate that Black English and Native American English dialect speakers have difficulty learning to read standard English (112, 123). These students' difficulties however, may have little to do with language interference.

Speakers of nonstandard English dialects tend to be from poor backgrounds. It is the many factors associated with having a poor background, not the students' nonstandard dialect that account for their lack of progress in reading. Educators' prejudicial attitudes against certain nonstandard English dialects interfere with students' learning. As noted above, many of them think that students who do not speak standard English are less intelligent; they have lower academic expectations for them; they evaluate both their oral and written work to be lower than comparable work of standard English-speaking students; and they are more likely to disapprove of them.

Teachers spend too much time correcting students' dialectic vocabulary, grammatical, and pronunciation "errors." There is considerable evidence that many teachers focus on dialectical differences that are not true errors rather than concentrate their efforts on improving students higher level skills and relate to them in unproductive ways (114, 115, 119, 120, 124).

2. *Competency in oral standard English is necessary for students to learn to write standard English.* Most experts in the field agree that it is not necessary for students to be able to speak standard English in

order to write standard English. While nonstandard forms of English intrude in students writing when they are first learning to write standard English, the longer students remain in school the fewer nonstandard English forms they use. That may be because writing is not speech written down.

3. ***Standard English is necessary for vocational success and in other areas in which nonstandard dialect speakers are branded as uneducated and ill-prepared*** (61, 64, 70). Many individuals believe that community attitudes are difficult if not impossible to change quickly. And they argue that schools should prepare students to succeed in the meantime. The following quotation typifies this line of thinking.

> There are many dialects in every language, but the standard form is that which is acceptable for purposes of state, business, or other everyday transactions. It is the official language of the country, and anyone who is successful in that country uses it. Those who use the nonstandard language are forever relegated to the most menial jobs and stations in life...If blacks are prepared to accept the hypothesis of 'black English,' then they ought to be prepared to accept the relegation to 'black jobs. If their preparation is second class, their lives will be second class. (71, p. 318, 320)

It is true that many members of our society are prejudiced against certain nonstandard English dialects. However, the solution to the problem is to combat discrimination, not accommodate and acquiesce to it. Students who want to learn to speak standard English because of the advantages it offers in the biased world in which they will live and work can learn to do so. After all, it is the language of instruction in school and the medium of communication outside of school.

Special educators have an important role to play in helping nonstandard English speakers. They should be correcting discrimination against nonstandard English dialects and helping students deal effectively with the discrimination they experience. They should not be encouraging students to acquiesce to it. As Dean & Fowler suggested quite some time ago:

> Previously, people who have applied for a job have been judged on clothing and hair styles. These discriminations have been lessened by change of public opinion. Then, people were judged on the color of their skin or their sex. These prejudices, while still present, are being lessened with the 'help' of legislation...White middle-class society has reexamined its values in the previously mentioned areas of hair style, clothing, race and sex. Surely that society can have its eyes opened once again. (59, p. 305-306)

When I ask myself whether there is any value to teaching students to speak standard English besides avoiding discrimination in the community and whether encouraging students to speak standard English will enable society to continue to discriminate against nonstandard English speakers I am convinced that we should not do so. I believe that as long as students can understand spoken and written standard English, they should be allowed or even encouraged to express themselves in their own dialects whenever they wish to do so (58, 59). The following are some reasons why.

Efforts to teach students to speak standard English do not work. There is considerable evidence that highly motivated individuals can learn standard English if they are given intensive instruction and interact on a frequent basis with standard English speakers. However, the way students are taught to speak standard English in school does not produce an increase in the frequency or correctness of students use of standard English in the classroom, much less outside of school (57, 62, 66, 70).

Teaching students standard English before they are completely fluent in their original dialects may stunt their language development. As Kochman wrote many years ago, switching from one dialect to another "does not develop the child's ability to use language beyond what he is already capable of doing... It is concerned with *how* the child says something rather than *how well* he says it" (65, p. 91).

Acceptance and appreciation of nonstandard dialects by schools and teachers improves students self-esteem.

"Black children must be educated to learn and believe that deviation from the normative pattern of standard English is not an indication that they are abnormal. They must be helped to understand that these negative social and psychological views have resulted and can continue to result in low self-esteem, identity crisis, and self-hatred. An appreciation of black habits, values, and goals is essential for black children to develop a positive black self-identity. The issue of black English is a 'good' place to start. Whites should not become reference points for how black children are to speak and behave." (58, p. 215)

It is not possible to encourage students to learn a second dialect without also communicating that their way of speaking is less desirable. As an English teacher put it:

No matter how carefully I explained my purpose and assured them that I was not judging their parents, grandparents, race, or culture... my students still resented my correcting them although most of the time they accepted my corrections in good humor. (69, p. 49)

Teaching standard English to nonstandard dialect speakers is a form of cultural subjugation. Nonstandard English speaking students and their teachers often have different perceptions of the implications of standard English. Teachers tend to view it as a way to learn more effectively and get ahead in the real world; students often view it as talking white, denying their heritage, and giving in to the European American power structure (67, 119).

I felt the oppressive nature of having my way of speaking criticized in school. And, like many other kids I resisted my teachers efforts to "help me." The junior high school that I attended in Brooklyn taught standard English. My English teachers were always correcting the way I spoke. At least it seemed that way to me. No dese, dem, and dose; no double negatives, no prepositions at the end of a sentence; don't say he don't, say he doesn't; don't say can I, say may I; don't say I will, say I shall; don't say I'll bring it wit me, say I will take it with me; don't say dem guys, say those boys; and so on. It was worse when we wrote. There were even more rules about commas, and hyphens, and preposition, and phrases, and clauses, and diagraming sentences, and so on. It seemed like my teachers didn't care what I said or wrote, only how I said and wrote it.

I never could see why the rules were so important. No one in my family or my neighborhood spoke or wrote that way. I didn't think that I should have to either. So I rebelled in junior high school and I rebelled in senior high school. At Harvard, I allowed myself to learn a little about writing standard English . But, I never learned how to use commas correctly, I continued to use contractions, and I made it a point to put prepositions anywhere I wanted to, even at the end of sentences if I felt like it.

My publications are all in standard English. But it's not my doing. Although I know that editors will add the commas where they belong, spell out contraction, and rewrite sentences so that they don't end with prepositions, I still submit my manuscripts the way I like them. And, in honor of the guys I grew up with and my New Yorkese-speaking parents, grandparents, aunts and uncle, I make sure that at least a few sentences end in prepositions and a few contractions are left in.

I had another experience that brought language bias home to me. I don't know how it works now, but back in the days when I first started teaching a New York State teaching credential wasn't good enough to teach in the New York City school system. I needed to pass the test given by the New York City Board of Education. I took the test which consisted of standing in front of an empty classroom and and teaching a lesson to an imaginary class. At the end of the lesson the examiner who was seated at the back of the room praised the content and format of my presentation; then he told me I had not passed the exam because I had a heavy Brooklyn accent. Ain't that something? Because of my accent I didn't get a license to teach kids in New York City, most of whom had even thicker accents than I had since I had been exposed to a lot of standard English speech at Harvard and had been required to take a speech class to correct my accent as part of my teacher preparation graduate program.

Shortly after I had completed the first draft of this book, the Oakland, California School District passed its now famous resolution on Ebonics, inadvertently, unintentionally, and unfortunately placing the issue of dialect into the same political arena as bilingual education. Hundreds of newspaper and magazine articles and television segments were devoted to the pro's and con's of their resolution. I did not read or hear all of these commentaries. However, among the ones I did read or hear, very few commentators had actually read the resolution and almost none of them referred to even one of the research studies reported here. Perhaps most important, the critics of the policy failed to recognize the fact that although the Oakland School Board was validating Ebonics, its goal was to use Ebonics to enable students to become fluent standard English speakers. That was what these critics wanted.

It seems that every time black folks decide to do something to improve their lives it becomes a political issue. Ain't that the truth!

REFERENCES

These references describe education in South Africa under the Afrikaner regime.

1. Freer, D. (1993). the residuals of apartheid: Impediments to teacher development in South Africa. In G. K. Verma (Ed.). *Inequality and Teacher Education: An International Perspective.* New York: Falmer Press.
2. Herman, H. D. (1992). South Africa. In Cookson, P. W. Jr., Sandovnik, A. R. & Semel, S. F. *International Handbook of Educational Reform.* New York: Greenwood Press.
3. Louw, W. J. (1988). Inservice upgrading of black teachers' qualifications in South Africa. In Sharp, D,. K. (Ed.) *International Perspectives on Teacher Education.* Routledge: London. p. 60.
4. Moodley, K. (1989). Educational ideologies and political control. In Yogev, A. & Tomlinson, S. (Eds.) *International Perspectives on Education and Society.* Greenwich, Connecticut: JAI Press.

Inequalities in the Israeli education system are the focus of these references.

5. Adler, C. (1989). Israeli education addressing dilemmas caused by pluralism: A sociological perspective. In Krauz, E., & Glanz, D. (Eds.) *Education in a Comparative Context: Studies of Israeli Society.* Vol IV New Brunswick, NJ: Transaction Publishers.
6. Masemann, V. L. The right to education for multicultural development: Canada and Israel. In Tarrow, N. B. (1987). *Human Rights and Education.* New York: Pergamon Press.
7. Mar'i, S. K. (1989). Arab education in Israel. In Krauz, E., & Glanz, D. (Eds.) *Education in a Comparative Context: Studies of Israeli Society.* Vol IV New Brunswick, NJ: Transaction Publishers.
8. Shavit, Y. (1989). Tracking and ethnicity in Israeli secondary education. In Krauz, E., & Glanz, D. (Eds.) *Education in a Comparative Context: Studies of Israeli Society.* Vol IV New Brunswick, NJ: Transaction Publishers.

These references discuss the role of education in assimilating indigenous cultures to dominant cultures.

9. Rust, V. D. (1992). Norway. In Cookson, P. W. Jr., Sandovnik, A. R. & Semel, S. F. *International Handbook of Educational Reform.* New York: Greenwood Press.
10. Hinckling-Hudson, A., & McMeniman, M. (1993). Beyond tokenism: Multiculturalism and teacher education in Australia. In G. K. Verma (Ed.).Inequality and Teacher Education: An International Perspective. New York: Falmer Press.

This publication contains the quote about the mainstream bias of the special education system.

11. Federal Regional Resource Center. (1991). *Exploring the Education issues of Cultural Diversity.* Lexington, KY: Interdisciplinary Human Development Institute, University of Kentucky. p. 5-7.

The importance of culturally appropriate special education services is detailed with in the following references.

12. Ford, B. A. (1995). (Ed.) *Multiple Voices for Ethnically Diverse Exceptional Learners.* Reston, VA: Council for Exceptional Children.
13. Ford, B. A., Obiakor, F. E., & Patton, M. (1995). *Effective Education of African American Exceptional Learners: New Perspectives.* Austin, TX: Pro-Ed.
14. Garcia, S. B. (1994) (Ed.) *Addressing Cultural and Linguistic Diversity in Special Education: Issues and Trends.* Reston, VA: Council for Exceptional Children.
15. Grossman, H. (1995). *Educating Hispanic Students: Implications for Instruction, classroom Management, Counseling, and Assessment.* 2nd Ed. Springfield, IL: Thomas.
16. Grossman H. (1995). *Special Education in a Diverse Society.* Boston: Allyn & Bacon.
17. Jones, R. L. (1976). *Mainstreaming and the Minority Child.* Reston, VA: Council for Exceptional Children.
18. Serwata, T., Dove, T., & Hodges, W. (1986). Black students in special education: Issues and implications for community involvement. *Negro Educational Review,* 37 (1), 17-26.

This reference reports ethnic differences in teachers evaluations of the importance of multicultural competencies.

19. Franklin, M. E., & James, J. (1997). *Are Special and General Education Teachers Likely to Provide Culturally Relevant Instruction?* Paper presented at the annual conference of the Council for Exceptional Children, New Orleans, January, 1997.

The unmet contextual problems of immigrant, refugee migrant, rural, and homeless children and adolescents with disabilities are detailed in the following references.

20. Heflin, L. J., & Rudy, K. (1991). *Homeless and in Need of Special Education.* Reston, Va: Council for Exceptional children.
21. Helge, D. (1984). The state of the art of rural special education. *Exceptional Children,* 50, 294-305.
22. Helge, D. (1989). *Rural Family-Community Partnerships: Resources.* ERIC ED 320 736.
23. Helge, D. (1991). *Rural, Exceptional, At Risk.* Reston, VA: Council for Exceptional Children.

24. Ken. (1986). *Neediest of the Needy: Special Education for Migrants. Harvesting the Harvesters. Book 8*. ERIC ED 279 473. Leadership for Special Education. A Conversation with Robert R. Davila. (1989). *Education of the Handicapped*, September 13, 28.

25. National Council on Disabilities. (1989). *The Education of Students with Disabilities: Where Do We Stand?* Washington, DC: Author.

26. Russell, S. C., & Williams, E. U. (1988). Homeless handicapped children: A special education perspective. *Children's Environments Quarterly*, 5(1), 3-7.

The educational situations in China and Tibet are discussed in this reference.

27. Postiglione, G. A. (1992). The implication of modernization for the education of China's national minorities. In Hayhoe, R. (Ed.) *Education and Modernization: The Chinese Experience*. New York: Pergamon Press.

These references discuss the large number of limited English proficient students in the United States.

28. Education of the Handicapped Act Amendments of 1990, (Individuals with Disabilities Education Act (20 U. S. C., Sections 1400-1485).

29. Woodrow, K. A. (1988). *Measuring Net Immigration to the United States: The Emigrant Population and Recent Emigration Flows*. Paper presented at the annual meeting of the Population Association of America, New Orleans.

The right of LEP students with disabilities to a linguistically appropriate education is the focus of the following references.

30. Bilingual Education Act of 1968.

31. Civil Rights Act of 1964.

32. *Dyrcia S. st al. v. Board of Education of the City of New York* (1979). 79 c. 2562 (E.D.N.Y.).

33. Equal Educational Opportunities Act of 1972.

34. Education of All Handicapped Children Act of 1974 (PL 94-142).

35. *Lau v. Nichols* (1974). 414 U.S. 563.

36. Rehabilitation Act of 1973.

Bilingual education and bilingual special education approaches are the focus of the following references.

37. Baca, L. M., & Cervantes, H. (1989). *The Bilingual Special Education Interface*. 2nd Ed. Columbus, OH: Merrill.

38. Cummins, J. (1984). *Bilingualism and Special Education: Issues in Assessment and Pedagogy*. San Diego: College Hill Press.

39. Olsen, L. (1988). *Crossing the Schoolhouse Border: Immigrant Students and the California Public Schools*. San Francisco: California Tomorrow.

54   *Ending Discrimination in Special Education*

40. Garcia, R. L. (1982). *Teaching in a Pluralistic Society: Concepts, Models, Strategies.* New York: Harper & Row.

This reference documents the shortage of bilingual special educators personnel preparation programs.

41. Medina, M. A. (1987). *Teacher Training Programs in Bilingual Special Education.* Unpublished masters thesis, San Diego State University, San Diego, CA.

The effects of the shortage of bilingual special educators and psychologists are documented in the following publication.

42. First, J. M., & Carrera, J. W. (1988). *New Voices: Immigrant Students in the Public Schools.* Boston: National Coalition of Advocates for Students.

The following references describe English as a second language techniques with students with disabilities and their effectiveness.

43. Cloud, N. (1988). *ESL in Special Education.* ERIC ED 303 044.
44. Cloud, N. (1990). Planning and implementing an English as a second language program. In A. L. Carrasquillo & R. E. Baecher (Eds.), *Teaching the Bilingual Special Education Student.* Norwood, NJ: Ablex.
45. Duran, E. (1985). Teaching fundamental reading in context to severely retarded and severely autistic adolescents of limited English proficiency. *Adolescence,* 20(78), 433-440.
46. Spolsky, B. (1988). Bridging the gap: A general theory of second language learning. *TESOL Quarterly,* 22, 377-396.

References that discuss sheltered English approaches and their effectiveness are listed below.

47. Chamot, A. U., & O'Malley, J. M. (1986). *A Cognitive Academic Language Learning Approach: An ESL Content-Based Curriculum.* Rosslyn, VA: National Clearinghouse for Bilingual Education.
48. Crandall, J. (Ed.). (1987). ESL *Through Content Area Instruction: Mathematics, Science, Social Studies.* Englewood Cliffs, NJ: Prentice-Hall..
49. Gersten, R., & Woodward, J. (1985). A case for structured immersion. *Educational Leadership,* 43(1), 75-79.
50. Northcutt, M., & Watson, D. (1986). *Sheltered English Teaching Handbook.* San Marcos, CA: AM Graphics & Printing.

The following references document the linguistically inappropriate special education services provided to LEP students who are not placed in bilingual programs.

51. Cegelka, P. T., Lewis, R., & Rodriguez, A. M. (1987). Status of educational services to handicapped students with limited English proficiency: Report of a

statewide study in California. *Exceptional Children,* 54, 220-227.

52. Harris, K. C., Rueda, R. S., & Supanchek, P. (1990). A descriptive study of literacy events in secondary special education programs in linguistically diverse schools. *Remedial and Special Education,* 11(4), 20-28.
53. Ortiz, A. A., & Wilkinson, C. Y. (1989). Adapting IEP's for limited English proficient students. *Academic Therapy,* 24(5), 555-568.

Various opinions about how special educators and regular educators should view and react to dialect differences are included in the following references.

54. Adger, C. T., Wolfram, W., & Detwyler, J. (1993). New roles for special educators in language differences. *Teaching Exceptional Children,* In press.
55. Adger, C. T., Wolfram, W., Detwyler, J., & Harry, B. (1993) Confronting dialect minority issues in special education: Reactive and proactive perspectives. *Proceedings of OBEMLA Research Conference.* Washington, DC: Government Printing Office.
56. Adler, S. (1987). Bidialectalism: Mandatory or elective? *Asha,* 29(1), 41-44.
57. Ash, S. & Myhill, J. (1983). *Linguistic Correlates of Interethnic Conflict.* Philadelphia: University of Pennsylvania, Linguistics Laboratory.
58. Davis, B. G., & Armstrong, H. (1981). The impact of teaching Black English on self-image and achievement. *Western Journal of Black Studies,* 5(3), 208-218.
59. Dean, M. B., & Fowler, E. D. (1974). An argument for appreciation of dialect differences in the classroom. *Journal of Negro Education,* 43(3), 302-309.
60. Farr, M. (1986). Language, culture, and writing: Sociolinguistic foundations of research on writing. In E. Z. Rothkopf (Ed.), *Review of Research on Education* No. 13. 195-223.
61. Ferguson, A. M. (1982). A case for teaching standard English to Black students. *English Journal,* 71(3), p. 38-40.
62. Graff, D., Labov, W., & Harris, W. (1983). *Testing Listeners' Reactions to Phonological Markers of Ethnic Identity: A New Method for Sociolinguistic Research.* Paper presented at the annual meeting of the New Ways of Analyzing Variations in English, Montreal.
63. Harris-Wright, K. (1987). The challenge of educational coalescence: Teaching nonmainstream English-speaking students. *Journal of Childhood Communication Disorders,* 11(1), 209-215.
64. Hochel, S. S. (1983). *A Position Paper on Teaching the Acquisition of the Mainstream Dialect in Kindergarten and Elementary School.* ERIC ED 238 060.
65. Kochman, T. (1969). Culture and communication; Implications for Black English in the classroom. *Florida Foreign Language Reporter,* Spring/Summer, 89-92, 172-174.
66. Labov, W., & Harris, W. (1983). *De facto Segregation of Black and White Vernacular.* Paper presented at the annual meeting of the New Ways of Analyzing Variations in English, Montreal.
67. Lipscomb, D. (1978). Perspectives on dialects in black students' writing. *Curriculum Review,* 17(3), 167-169.

68. Padak, N. D. (1981). The language and educational needs of children who speak Black English. *Reading Teacher,* 35(2), 144-151.
69. Simmons, E. A. (1991). Ain't we never gonna study no grammar? *English Journal,* 80(8), 48-5.
70. Taylor, O. L. (1986). A cultural and communicative approach to teaching standard English as a second dialect. In O. L. Taylor (Ed.), *Treatment of Communication Disorders in Culturally and Linguistically Diverse Populations.* San Diego: College-Hill Press.
71. Thomas, E. W. (1978). English as a second language–For whom? *The Crisis,* 85(9), 318-320.

Legal requirements regarding non standard English dialects is the focus of the following reference.

72. *Martin Luther King Junior Elementary School Children versus Ann Arbor School District Board of Education,* 451 F. Supplement 1324 (Michigan 1978); 463 F. Supplement 1027 (Michigan 1978); No. 7-71861, Slip Op. (Michigan, July 12, 1979).

The following references document dialect bias in teachers' evaluations of non standard English speaking students.

73. DeMeis, D., & Turner, R. (1978). Effects of students' race, physical attractiveness, and dialect on teachers' evaluations. *Contemporary Educational Psychology,* 3, 77-86.
74. Elliot, S. N., & Argulewicz, E. N. (1983). The influence of student ethnicity on teachers' behavior ratings of normal and learning disabled children. *Hispanic Journal of Behavioral Sciences,* 5(3), 337-345.
75. Granger, R. E., Mathews, M., Quay, L. C., & Verner, R. (1977). Teacher judgments of communication effectiveness of children using different speech patterns. *Journal of Educational Psychology,* 69 (6), 793-796.
76. Haller, E. J., & Davis, S. A. (1980). Does socioeconomic status bias the assignment of elementary school students to reading groups? *American Educational Research Journal,* 17 (40, 409-418.
77. Marwit, K., Marwit, S., & Walker, E. (1978). Effects of student race and physical attractiveness on teachers' judgments of transgressions. *Journal of Educational Psychology,* 70, 911-915.
78. Scheinfeld, D. R. (1983). Family relationships and school achievement among boys of lower-income urban black families. *American Journal of Orthopsychiatry,* 53 (1), 127-143.
79. Taylor, J. B. (1983). Influence of speech variety on teachers' evaluation of reading comprehension. *Journal of Educational Psychology,* 75 (5), 662-667.
80. Tobias, S., Cole, C., Zibrin, M., & Bodlakova, V. (1981). *Bias in the Referral of Children to Special Services.* ERIC ED 208 637.

The following researchers found that assessing nonstandard dialect speakers in standard English does not produce biased results.

81. Desberg, P., Marsh, G., Schneider, L. A., & Duncan-Rose, C. (1979). The effects of social dialect on auditory sound blending and word recognition. *Contemporary Educational Psychology*, 4, 14-144.
82. Frentz, T. S. (1971). Children's comprehension of standard and Negro non standard English sentences. *Speech Monographs*, 38, 10-16.
83. Hockman, C. H. (1973). Black dialect reading tests in the urban schools. *Reading Teacher*, 26, 581-583.
84. Nolen, P. (1972). Reading of non-standard dialect materials, a study at grades two and four. *Child Development*, 43, 1092-1097.

The references listed below describe bias resulting from assessing nonstandard dialect speakers with standard English procedures and how to avoid it.

85. Baratz, J. (1969). *Language and Cognitive Assessment of Negro Children: Assumptions and Research Needs*. Paper presented at the annual meeting of the American Speech and Hearing Association, Washington, DC.
86. Benmaman, V., & Schenck, S. J. (1986). *Language Variability: An Analysis of Language Variability and Its Influence upon Special Education Assessment*. ERIC ED 296 532.
87. Bliss, L. S., & Allen, D. V. (1981). Black English responses on selected language tests. *Journal of Communication Disorders*, 14, 225-233.
88. Bryen, D. N. (1976). Speech-sound discrimination ability on linguistically unbiased tests. *Exceptional Children*, 42(4), 195-201.
89. Burke, S. M., Pflaum, S. W., & Knafle, J. D. (1982). The influence of black English on diagnosis of reading in learning disabled and normal readers. *Journal of Learning Disabilities*, 15(1), 19-22.
90. Byrd, M. L. , & Williams, H. S. (1981). *Language Attitudes and black Dialect: An Assessment. (1) Language Attitudes in the Classroom. (2) A Reliable Measure of Language Attitude*. ERIC ED 213 062.
91. Cartledge, G., Stupay, D., & Kaczala, C. (1984). *Formal Language Assessment of Handicapped and Nonhandicapped Black Children*. ERIC ED 250 348.
92. Evans, J. S. (1972). Word-pair discrimination and imitation abilities of preschool Spanish-speaking children. *Journal of Learning Disabilities*, 7(9), 49-56.
93. Fisher, D., & Jablon, A. (1984). An observation of the phonology of black English speaking children. In Queens College Department of Communication Arts and Sciences. *Working Papers in Speech-Language Pathology and Audiology*. Flushing, Queens: City University of New York.
94. Harber, J. R. (1980). Issues in the assessment of language and reading disorders in learning disabled children. *Learning Disability Quarterly*, 3(4), 20-28.
95. Hemingway, B. L., Montague J. C. Jr., & Bradley, R. H. (1981). Preliminary data on revision of a sentence repetition test for language screening with black first grade children. *Language, Speech, and Hearing Services in Schools*, 12, 145-152.
96. Jensen, L. J. (1976). Dialect. In P. A. Allen (Ed.), *Findings of Research in Miscue*

Analyses: Classroom Implications. Urbana, IL: National Council of Teachers of English.

97. Mackler, B., & Holman, D. (1976). Assessing, packaging, and delivery: Tests, testing, and race. *Young Children,* 31(5), 351-364.

98. Musselwhite, C. R. (1983). Pluralistic assessment in speech-language pathology: Use of dual norms in the placement process. *Language, Speech, and Hearing Services in Schools,* 14, 29-37.

99. Norris, M. K., Juarez, M. J. & Perkins, M. N.(1989). Adaptation of a screening test for bilingual and bidialectal populations. *Language, Speech, and Hearing Services in Schools,* 20(4), 381-390.

100. Ramstad, V. V., & Potter, R. E. (1974). Differences in vocabulary and syntax usage between Nez Perce Indian and white kindergarten children. *Journal of Learning Disabilities,* 7(8), 35-41.

101. Rivers, L. W. (1978). The influence of auditory, visual, and language discrimination skills on the standardized test performance of Black children. *Journal of NonWhite Concerns,* 6(3), 134-140.

102. Ross, H. W. (1979). Wepman Test of Auditory Discrimination: What does it discriminate *Journal of School Psychology,* 17(1), 47-54.

103. Seymour, H. N., & Seymour, C. M. (1977). A therapeutic model for communicative disorders among children who speak Black English vernacular. *Journal of Speech and Hearing Disorders,* 42, 238-246.

104. Thurmond, V. B. (1977). The effect of Black English on the reading test performance of high school students. *Journal of Educational Research,* 70(3), 160-163.

105. Vaughn-Cooke, F. B. (1980). Evaluation the language of black English speakers: Implications of the Ann Arbor decision. In M. F. Whileman (Ed.), *Reactions to Ann Arbor: Vernacular Black English and Education.* Arlington VA: Center for Applied Linguistics.

106. Wartella, A. B., & Williams, D. (1982). *Speech and Language Assessment of Black and Bilingual Children.* ERIC ED 218 914.

107. Weiner, F. D., Lewnay, L., & Erway, E. (1983). Measuring language competence of Black American English. *Journal of Speech and Hearing Disorders,* 48, 76-84.

108. Williams R. L., & Rivers, L. W. (1972). *The Use of Standard Versus Non-Standard English in the Administration of Group Tests to Black Children.* Paper presented at the annual meeting of the American Psychological Association, Honolulu.

The following references provide descriptions of expected differences that may occur in responses on some standardized tests given to speakers of nonstandard dialects.

109. Deyhle, D. (1985). Testing among Navajo and Anglo students: Another consideration of cultural bias. *Journal of Educational Equity and Leadership,* 5, 119-131.

110. Hunt, B. C. (1974-1975). Black dialect and third and fourth graders' performance on the Gray Oral Reading Test. *Reading Research Quarterly,* 10, 103-123.

The following references shed light on the relationship between nonstandard dialects and reading.

111. Anastasiow, N. J., Levine-Hanes, M. , & Hanes, M. L. (1982). *Language & Reading Strategies for Poverty Children.* Baltimore: University Park Press.
112. Barth, J. L. (1979). Nonstandard English and Native Students: When is a difference a disability? *British Columbia Journal of Special Education,* 3,(4), 357-363.
113. Bougere, M. B. (1981). Dialect and reading disabilities. *Journal of Research and Development in Education,* 14(4), 67-73.
114. Collins, J. (1988). Language and class in minority education. *Anthropology and Education Quarterly,* 19 (4), 299-326.
115. Dandy, E. B. (1988). *Dialect Differences: Do They Interfere?* ERIC ED 294 240.
116. Gibson, E., & Levin, H. (1975). *The Psychology of Reading.* Cambridge, MA: MIT Press.
117. Lass, B. (1980). Improving reading skills: The relationship between the oral language of black English speakers and their reading achievement. *Urban Education,* 14(4), 437-447.
118. Levine-Hanes, M., & Hanes, M. L. (1979). *Developmental Differences in Dialect, Function Word Acquisition and Reading.* Paper presented at the annual meeting of the International Reading Association, Atlanta.
119. McGinnis, J., & Smitherman, G. (1978). Sociolinguistic conflict in the schools. *Journal of Non-White Concerns in Personnel and Guidance,* 6(2), 87-95.
120. Pflaum, S. W. (1978). Minority student language and reading acquisition. In S. E. Pflaum-Connor (Ed.), *Aspects of Reading Education.* Berkeley, CA: McMutchan.
121. Simons, H. (n.d.). *Black Dialect Interference and Classroom Interaction.* Berkeley, CA: School of Education, University of California.
122. Sims, R. (1976). What we know about dialects and reading. In P. D. Allen & D. J. Watson (Eds.), *Findings if Research in Miscue Analysis: Classroom Implications.* Urbana IL: National Council of Teachers of English.
123. Strand, C. M. (1979). *Bidialectalism and Learning to Read.* Unpublished doctoral dissertation, Ann Arbor: University of Michigan.
124. Washington, V. M., & Miller-Jones, D. (1989). Teacher interaction with non standard English speakers during reading instruction. *Contemporary Educational Psychology,* 14(3), 280-312.

Chapter 4

OBSTACLES TO CHANGE AND SOLUTIONS

We know both who the students are that are treated unjustly by the special education system and the specific ways that they are treated unfairly. What is more, we have the know-how and the resources to correct the problem. Nevertheless, many special educators, administrators, and psychologists continue to contribute to the problem rather than to its solution. I would like to focus on five of the many reasons why many special educators resist learning about students' cultural, contextual, and linguistic characteristics and why many of those who do have this knowledge are nevertheless reluctant to adapt their methods to these students' needs. These reasons include the lack of diversity among special educators, their prejudicial attitudes, their reluctance to rock the boat because of the risks involved, their unwillingness to expend the energy involved in teaching in a multicultural manner, and their lack of preparedness for working with the diverse group of students in our special education programs.

UNREPRESENTATIVE SPECIAL EDUCATORS

The teachers who staff our special education programs are not representative of the students they teach (1-5). Teachers from poor, non-middle-class or non-European American backgrounds are scarce and becoming more scarce. Although 32 percent of students in special education programs are non-European Americans, only 14 percent of their teachers are non-European Americans. The most recent statistics indicate that the disproportionality in the ethnic background of special education teachers will be maintained if not increased in the near future. Eighty-eight percent of students enrolled in special education personnel preparation programs are European Americans; only 6.6 percent are African American and only 3.1 percent are Hispanic American. (The ethnic breakdown of students enrolled in special education personnel preparation programs in 1995 was: Asian American 401, African American 3,944, Hispanic American 1,418, Native American 260, European American 33,336, unknown 6,358). In addition, in comparison to European American special educators, non-European American special educators are significantly more likely to plan to leave the field.

Professors of education bear some of the responsibility for the lack of diversity among our teachers. With some exceptions, professors spend little time recruiting nonmiddle-class and non-European American students into their teacher preparation programs. When they do recruit nonmiddle-class and non-European American students, they tend to choose students who, like them, have adopted a middle-class European American way of life. And, they often turn off many of the students who have not assimilated to the mainstream culture by using culturally and contextually inappropriate instructional, classroom management, and assessment approaches.

Special education professors must recruit into their teacher preparation programs individuals who are devoted to improving the education of all students, non-European American, poor, migrant, immigrant, and rural, students as well as middle-class European American students. The recruitment of bilingual individuals, non-European Americans, and European Americans who because of own life experiences understand and appreciate students' cultural, contextual, and linguistic characteristics should be given special attention.

UNMOTIVATED AND PREJUDICED SPECIAL EDUCATORS

During my 40 years in special education, I have known a great many caring teachers and teachers-in-training who were dedicated to helping all children and struggling to achieve that goal. And, I am sure that there are thousands more like them that I have never met. Unfortunately, many other special educators do not want to know that their approaches are culturally, contextually, and linguistically inap-

The situation in the university where I teach is a good example. A number of my colleagues who were awarded federal funds to provide scholarships to "minority" and/or bilingual students in order to increase the number of non-European American and bilingual special educators asked me what I did to recruit students for the programs I ran. When I told them that we sent letters to the more than one thousand school buildings in our service area, made presentations about our program in the local school districts and at meetings of the county education administrators, interviewed candidates at sites off campus that were convenient to their places of residence or work, followed up every inquiry with at least a telephone call, asked graduates of our program to contact prospective students to encourage them to apply, and so on, they thanked me, but implemented few, if any, of my suggestions. The end result in many cases was that their minimal recruitment efforts were unsuccessful. And, they met their quotas with students who were technically "minorities" because they were Jewish, Japanese-American, and so on, but not actually members of underrepresented groups; or students who spoke German, French or other languages that were not needed by the limited proficient English elementary and secondary students in the university's service area; or just "warm European American bodies" who were more interested in the tuition waivers the programs offered than in serving non-European American and limited English proficient students with disabilities. And to protect themselves and continue to receive the funds, they provided misleading information to the people in Washington who monitored whether the programs were achieving their objectives.

propriate for some of their students. These educators may be comfortable with their accustomed way of doing things and/or unwilling to face the anxiety of not knowing how to adapt their approaches to their students' individual needs. Many of them just care less about students whose skin color, socioeconomic, ethnic, contextual or linguistic backgrounds are different from their own than they care about students with whom they identify. As far as they are concerned, ignorance is bliss. These attitudes are understandable since they reflect the human condition. However, they are attitudes that must be corrected.

Some special educators believe that doing the right thing is not worth risking their relationships with colleagues or their job security. They are right about the risks they will run. The changes that are required in adapting traditional special education to the needs of the diverse students in our schools are threatening to those who wish to maintain the status quo. The community and educational forces arrayed against bilingual special education, Ebonics, multicultural special education, nonbiased assessment, and so on are formidable. It is risky to take on an establishment that is satisfied with the status quo or unwilling to change things because of politics. However, it is a risk that special educators are obligated to take because they have assumed the responsibility for their students' educations.

Finally, some special educators are unwilling to commit themselves to the additional time and effort that they think would be involved in adapting their approaches to their students' diverse needs. They too are partially right. Adapting special education methods to students' diverse needs would require considerable work on their part, but not extra work. They would be merely doing what is necessary to perform their job the way it should be done. My personal belief is that these attitudes reflect the self-centeredness that all of us must battle against to one degree or another.

Many special educators' attitudes about diversity reflect the prejudices prevalent in society. One prejudicial attitude some educators have is their belief that the European American culture that prevails in the United States is superior to the "disadvantaged or inferior" cultures from which many non-European American students or their parents emigrated. Special educators who believe this think that it would be a disastrous mistake for them to encourage students to maintain the inferior cultural characteristics that held back the progress of the countries from which they or their parents emigrated. Instead they maintain that they should encourage non-European American students and their parents to give up those cultural characteristics that have held back the progress of their native countries. As one person put it anonymously:

> People came to this country to better themselves. If their native cultures are so great, why did they have to immigrate? If they aren't willing to accept the val-

One of the ways I measure the effectiveness of the courses in diversity that I teach is to compare my students' responses at the outset and at the end of the semester to questions about how they think a variety of problematic classroom situations should be handled. When I do so, I repeatedly find that at the end of the course they are much more likely to believe that teachers should adapt their approaches to their students' individual needs. However, when I ask my students if they would actually make the adaptions they affirm are desirable, their answers are mixed. In general, they report that they have adapted or anticipate adapting many of their instructional techniques to their students' cultural, socioeconomic, contextual, and linguistic needs. That is unlikely to cause them problems. They are less willing to adapt their classroom management approaches to their students' individual needs because accepting certain kinds of behavior would make them very uncomfortable. And, they are extremely unlikely to adapt their assessment approaches to their students' characteristics because that would create major waves with their colleagues and administrators. As many of them put it, albeit apologetically, 'I wouldn't risk my job by refusing to administer a test even though I knew it was biased.'

Having been fired from or asked to leave a number of jobs when I was younger, I know that the threat they experience is real. However, when I think about the students who they are miseducating, I am not very sympathetic to their concerns.

ues that have helped the United States have the largest economy and the highest standard of living then they should return to the countries from which they came and settle for the limited opportunities they provide. (6, p.18)

This point of view is just another example of the prejudicial attitudes that non-European American students experience in our schools.

Believing that the European American middle-class culture that currently prevails in school is a superior culture, these special educators claim that students will learn more effectively if they assimilate to the learning and behavior styles that prevail in schools and use the school's values as a standard to judge themselves.

There is little evidence to support the hypothesis that students who assimilate learn more efficiently. In fact, there is evidence that the non-European students who are most likely to be well-adjusted and to succeed both academically and vocationally are not those who reject their ethnic identity, rather those who identify with their own ethnic group (7, 13-15, 21, 23, 24, 27-29, 30, 31).

The reasons why these students are better adjusted and more successful have not been well studied. Some possible explanations are:

- Students who have not assimilated bring the positive aspects of their cultures to the educational situation.

- Students who assimilate may substitute the poor attitudes toward school that characterize many European American students for the positive attitudes that prevail in their original culture.

- Students who maintain their cultural identity have more self-esteem and self-confidence than those who reject their cultural background.

- In comparison to monocultural students, bicultural students have a larger repertoire of learning strategies and coping techniques to apply to the tasks and challenges of school.

- Students who are attempting to assimilate may experience conflicts with their parents as well as identity conflicts, resentment, anger, and, rebelliousness, all of which can interfere with students' learning.

A second prejudicial notion that some special educators support is that adapting their approaches to individual students' will contribute to people wanting to follow different laws, operate on the basis of different values and moralities, and so on. This idea is embodied in the following statements:

> We cannot survive as a culture with different laws for different people. Everyone must pay taxes, serve in the army, respect private property and the rights of others regardless of where they were born or what religion they profess. (6, p. 10)

> Pluralism in our society has produced a moral climate that tells everyone to establish a sense of what is right and wrong *for you*. This trend has a way of blurring the limits of a moral code. In the educational arena this trend has produced a no-fault morality and relativistic values...Schools, if they are to survive,

must protect and articulate moral standards, ethical behavior, and historical principles of social cohesion. It is their function to teach the common beliefs that unite us as a free nation. (9, p. 15-16)

This idea seems patently illogical. These concerns are based on the incorrect assumption that persons who favor pluralistic approaches believe in complete cultural relativism. Pluralists typically recommend that diversity should be balanced against higher and universal values (8, 10, 18, 26). Two examples of this position follow.

Because each cultural group proceeds from a different context, we can never reach total agreement on the 'best' or most appropriate ways in which to lead our lives... Nevertheless, it should also be stressed that above and beyond all cultures there are human and civil rights that need to be valued and maintained by all people. These rights guarantee that all human beings are treated with dignity, respect, and equality. Sometimes the values and behaviors of a group so seriously challenge these values that we are faced with a dilemma to reject it or to affirm the diversity it represents. If the values we as human beings hold most dear are ultimately based on extending rights rather than negating them, we must decide on the side of those more universal values. (10, p. 278-279)

I believe in a form of cultural pluralism in which universal and particularistic values would be dialectically balanced against each other. In particular, I believe that the universal values of equality, freedom, and democracy, which are among the most important values that have been promulgated under the concept of common school, should be balanced against the particularistic values associated with the maintenance of cultural diversity. But the freedom of an individual must be restrained to the extent that it imposes detrimentally on the freedom of others. Unfortunately, this two-sided nature of cultural pluralism is rarely underlined and, as a consequence, it is sometimes misunderstood as license for runaway ethnicity, rather than as a way of avoiding such ethnocentric behavior. (8 p. 300-301)

The contention that accommodating to cultural differences in the classroom necessarily leads to having two or more national languages and different laws for different cultural groups is also incorrect. Instructing students in their native languages while they learn English, permitting them to work at their own pace, developing the kinds of interpersonal relationships with them that make them feel comfortable, allowing them to choose whether to behave competitively or cooperatively and so on does not necessarily lead to adopting two or more national languages, moral codes, or sets of laws.

Special educators who are prejudiced against their students or unwilling to adapt their approaches to their students for the reasons described above have many ways of rationalizing their resistances.

Adapting classroom approaches to students needs does not prepare them for the real world. Some special educators have convinced themselves that because the real world is not nearly as tolerant or as flexible as school, adapting educational approaches to students' individual characteristics and backgrounds does not prepare them to function effectively in the mainstream European American dominated society. They maintain that because employers and others require individuals to conform to mainstream expectations and norms, accommodating to students' culturally influenced behavior patterns, learning styles, communication styles, concepts of punctuality, and so on dooms them to be uncompetitive and disadvantaged in the real world. This is the same argument that some educators give to justify teaching students to speak standard English.

As I stated earlier, there is some truth to this concern. Americans do live in an imperfect society. Despite federal and state laws against discrimination, too many people with supervisory and administrative power over others continue to expect and insist that those over whom they have influence conform to their culturally determined standards. However, does that mean that educators should prepare their students to accept the prejudicial attitudes of these individuals? Again we must ask who has the right to decide whether students should be encouraged and helped to submit to such abuse, or to fight it—the students' teachers or the students themselves?

Many students do not want to replace their values, attitudes, learning and behavior styles and so on with those of the European American middle-class. Requiring them to do so can cause them to become angry, resentful, suspicious, and rebellious, and to tune out their teachers or drop out of school. If students believe that their culture is inferior or they agree that they should change their culturally determined ways of functioning they may suffer a loss of self-esteem and self-confidence. Even if students want to change, it may be too difficult to accomplish, since it is no easy task to change one's life-style and values.

There is a limited capability within each of us to modify the ethnic traits we absorb as children. We may change our accent or the way we smile but we cannot, intellectually or emotionally, change the multitude of traits that would have to be altered to change our basic ethnicity. (22, p. 20)

Even if students succeed in changing, their efforts can create serious problems and unwanted side effects. When non-European American students act in ways that are less natural to them than to European American middle-class students who are brought up from their earliest years to behave in these ways, they can become tense and nervous. And they may experience the guilt, shame, and anxiety that often results from rejecting one's culture. Students who assimilate may suffer the loss of friendship and outright hostility from peers who accuse them of trying to be "coconuts, oreos or bananas" (brown, black or yellow on the outside and white on the inside). This is especially likely to happen if there is movement within the students' culture toward increasing the groups' cultural pride or if there is a history of conflict and oppression between the students' ethnic group and the European American power structure.

There is little reason to assume that assimilation can work. It has been tried for years with very little success. This concern was expressed quite some time ago by one of the pioneers in the field of multicultural education.

Schools' past efforts to acculturate culturally different children have failed miserably. These children as a whole are still not being educated, and the school system cannot continue to ignore its ethical, legal, moral, and professional responsibilities to accommodate children as they are. It is highly presumptuous for any school system to assume the responsibilities of acculturating children when the potential emotional consequences of forced acculturation are so pernicious. If most educators realized the way in which they risk the mental health of culturally different children by insisting on acculturating them, they would look more favorably on their potential role in developing a culturally pluralistic society. (12, p. 555) .

It is impossible to accommodate educational approaches to the cultural needs of the many culturally different students found in any particular school system or often within a particular classroom.

Many people do not believe that educators can accommodate their methods and techniques to the different cultural groups with whom they work. Some of their reasons are included in the following quotation.

> My school district, the Los Angeles County School District, has over one hundred different language/culture groups. How can anyone be expected to know about all these different cultures, and how can anyone be expected to apply what they do know? From what I have been told during in-service training, what are appropriate teaching techniques for one group are inappropriate for another. How can I teach my Anglo students one way, my Latino students a second way, my Vietnamese students a third, my Korean students a fourth way, my Hmong, my Portuguese, etc., at the same time? Impossible! (6, p. 16)

These special educators are wrong. It is factually incorrect to assert that each culture requires a unique educational approach. Alternative methods of instructing students, assessing students, organizing classrooms and counseling parents are limited. For example, educators can encourage or require their students to work individually or in groups; they can motivate them through the use of competitive games or cooperative settings; they can allow them to work at their own pace or encourage them to work as quickly as possible; they can attempt to develop close personal relationships with them or maintain a "professional distance"; they can correct and criticize them in front of their peers or privately; they can encourage them to discuss controversial issues and express differences of opinion or emphasize similarities of experience and opinion; and they can teach abstract concepts or utilize methods which stress the concrete and learning by doing. Because educators are always choosing between alternatives as limited as those listed above, they can easily adapt their methodology to the cultural needs of their students.

To treat some students differently than others is discriminatory.
Some special educators argue that since all people are basically the same they should be treated the same. Not to do so, in their opinion is unfair and discriminatory.

While it is true that human beings are similar: they prefer success to failure, praise and recognition to criticism or condemnation, and acceptance and attention to rejection and inattention. However, peoples' behavior in these situations is influenced by different cultural veneers. They have different criteria for success. They find different forms of praise and recognition rewarding. They differ in terms of when, where, why, and how they are willing to accept criticism or condemnation. And they express acceptance and rejection in their own culturally determined ways. Therefore, if teachers expect all individuals to behave the same way and interpret everyone's behavior from a single culturally determined point of view, they may fail to respond to the unique needs of many of their students.

In addition, the result of treating all students the same may be that those who do not fit the model used by their teachers are treated in a discriminatory manner.

> When teachers ignore students' race and claim that they treat all children the same, they usually mean that their model of the ideal student is white and middle-class. (20, p. 54)

For example, Hilliard (19) advises that educators who believe that providing students the same instructional techniques, classroom management approaches and so on have the mistaken notion that they are treating them equally and being fair to them. However, they are not treating all students the same, but are dealing with some students in a culturally appropriate manner and others in a biased manner. Hilliard suggests that there is a more valid way of treating students the same which is to provide all students with culturally appropriate educational approaches. According to him, while this may make it appear that students are being treated differently, they are actually being treated the same and in a nondiscriminatory manner.

It would not be a good idea for professionals involved in educating non-European American students to use misleading and even prejudicial descriptions of their cultures.

Some special educators are convinced that attempting to be culturally relevant, can easily result in adapting their educational practices to misleading and outdated stereotypes and incorrect beliefs. Some teachers do accept outdated or fictionalized versions of their students' cultures and focus on the quaint or unusual aspects of their lifestyles. However, this suggests that educators should take great care to avoid these problems. It does not mean that they should not attempt to learn as much as they can about their students' cultural background. One of the most effective ways of combating such prejudice is to provide educators with accurate descriptions of the cultural, contextual, and linguistic characteristics of ethnic groups.

Cultural descriptions can lead to misleading over generalizations.

Some special educators are concerned that teachers may think that their knowledge of the typical cultural, contextual, and linguistics characteristics of a group is sufficient for them to understand an individual student or parent. The following statement expresses this concern.

> There are many common stereotypes of the Hispanic person such as never being on time, being deeply religious, etc. Those who work with Hispanics should be aware of this and guard against a generalized, stereotyped view of those they work with. This is not to say that a specific stereotype (like being deeply religious) may not apply to an individual. Rather, the individual should always be dealt with as a unique human being who may or may not exhibit certain attitudes, habits, and beliefs...Educators must recognize that children come to us from an infinitely varied array of backgrounds and not assume that all Hispanic students come from poor or Indian backgrounds. (6, p. 14)

The possibility of overgeneralization is an ever present danger. However, while it is extremely important to avoid misleading stereotypes and overgeneralizations about any group of students, such generalizations can be helpful. They can sensitize special educators, psychologists, and others who work in schools to the *possibility* that their students may have certain stereotypic attitudes, preferences, values, learning styles, and behavior patterns. However, they should never assume that their students will *necessarily* think and behave in these ways. It is as important to avoid relating to students on the basis of incorrect stereotypes as it is to avoid being insensitive to the influence students' ethnic characteristics have on their attitudes and behavior.

Treating groups of students differently can result in lower expectations and standards for them. It can also lead European Americans to retaliate against those who they believe are given preferential treatment.

These are valid concerns. In an attempt to be culturally, contextually, and linguistically relevant, some well-meaning special educators do lower their standards for students. However, these teachers are not following the advice of experts who caution them to maintain realistic standards and expectations for students and not assume that they will behave in an anti-social manner or achieve less than others while they educate them in a culturally appropriate manner.

UNDERPREPARED EDUCATORS

During my thirty-some-odd years as a professor, I have met some outstanding professors of special education, (especially when I attended the various symposia on diversity sponsored by the Council for Exceptional Children), who were dedicated to preparing their students to succeed with the diverse group of children with disabilities that attend our schools. While most of them were people of color, quite a few were European Americans like myself. Unfortunately, these committed professors are not in the majority. In general, professors of special education do not prepare teachers to work with the diverse group of students enrolled in our special education programs. Many special education professors pay lip service to preparing educators to succeed with our diverse groups of students. They claim that they include multicultural approaches in the courses they teach. But at best, they merely include one or two, occasionally three articles about multicultural education in their assigned readings, tell students not to be prejudiced, and let it go at that.

With few exceptions, professors do not select textbooks that have a multicultural approach for their courses. When they teach their students how to instruct, manage, counsel, and assess students they recommend the same techniques for all students. And, when they themselves instruct and assess their own students and manage their own classrooms, they use the same techniques with all students without regard to the diversity among them. Typically they use their same preferred teaching styles whether it be lecturing, cooperative learning, small group discussion, and so on over and over again, never thinking that their students' have different learning styles. They often take students' participation in class discussions into account when determining their grades (sometimes telling students in advance how many points classroom participation will be worth) even though some students may not wish to talk in class, and even though there is no evidence that talking in class is related to learning. They give all their students the same multiple choice, or short or long essay test, without thinking about the possibility of providing students with alternative ways of demonstrating their competency. They assess all students with timed tests, even though some students may not be able to demonstrate what they have accomplished in the course when they are rushed. They often deduct points or lower the grade they give to a paper that is turned in late, completely disregarding the fact that the context of the lives of some of their students may have prevented them from completing the assignment "on time." And so on.

This intolerable situation must change. First, we need to hire more non-European American professors who are more likely to be sensitive to and appreciative of the influence of cultural, linguistic, contextual, and gender factors on all students' learning and behavior (33). This will require paying more than lip service to faculty diversity and giving priority to hiring non-European American professors or European American professors with the required experience and knowledge. My experience indicates that this will be an unpopular policy among some faculties. However, it is an absolutely essential one.

Even if faculty attitudes were to change overnight, as of now, the number of non-European American special educators with doctorate degrees and doctoral students is insufficient to diversify our special education personnel preparation programs. Therefore, we must begin by recruiting more of them into our doctoral training programs. This will not be easy. In comparison to European American special educators, non-European American special educators' decisions about whether to pursue a doctorate degree are influenced by program support for tuition, books, and living expenses; the number of non-European Americans on the faculty, among the students in the program, and in the local community; the services available to non-European Americans; and the presence of organizations that concern themselves with the interests and issues of non-European Americans (34, 35). This suggests that universities and state and federal governments will have to provide the funding necessary to enable non-European Americans to engage in doctoral studies which in some cases might mean giving priority to providing financial assistance to non-European Americans. And they will have to attract them in sufficient numbers that they will feel welcome and comfortable, not isolated on university campuses.

Secondly, all professors of special education have to become knowledgeable about the ways in which teachers and professors can adapt their instructional, classroom management and assessment approaches to the specific different cultural, linguistic, and contextual characteristics of their students. Sensitivity to and appreciation of individual differences is a necessary first step, and, god knows a difficult one to achieve with higher education faculty. However, sensitivity is insufficient. As professors become knowledgeable about these differences and how to accommodate to them they must act on their knowledge in their own classrooms. This means modeling the kinds of behavior that their students need to learn.

To begin with, they must select textbooks that have a multicultural approach for their courses. Here are two examples of multicultural approaches. The first is an example of a multicultural discussion of cooperative learning. It is very different from the typical discussions in textbooks that never mention cultural, contextual, or gender influences on students' learning styles.

When students with disabilities learn in cooperative environments, typically interethnic relationships improve, students learn more, and feel better about themselves, their peers, and school. However, some students respond less positively than others to this cooperative approach. For example, African Americans, Filipino Americans, Hawaiian Americans, Hispanic Americans, and European American females tend to be brought up to expect and count on the help and the cooperation of others and to reciprocate in kind. European American males who are taught to rely only on themselves to accomplish their goals and deal with the challenges, difficulties and problems may react better to competitive and individualistic situations.

Ethnic groups also have different approaches to cooperation. When European Americans work cooperatively, everyone is supposed to do her or his share. Hispanic Americans, on the other hand, are less likely to be offended by a group member who does not do her or his share. The best qualified or most interested individuals do the bulk of the labor and assume that the others will contribute when their talents and interests are needed.

Female students tend to achieve more in single-sex cooperative learning situations than in mixed-sex cooperative groups. Females participate and lead less in mixed-gender groups. Although they tend to be the providers of assistance, they are rejected by males when they ask for assistance. In addition, in mixed-sex cooperative groups females often revert to a pattern of not interacting with male students, allowing males to dominate them, and viewing themselves as less helpful, less important, and less visible. Males may actually learn more and perform better than females in cooperative mixed-sex groups because they often ignore females, contribute most of the ideas, do most of the talking, and typically function as the group leaders. Sometimes, the experiences of some African American students in mixed-ethnic cooperative groups is similar. This happens when European American students assume the leadership roles and African American children assume more subservient roles.

Females and African American students can benefit from mixed-gender or mixed-ethnic cooperative groups when they have been given advanced training so they can function as expert/leaders of the group. Providing these students with prior experience with the group task so they are familiar with what is to be learned and preparing all students in the group to function in a more egalitarian manner are also helpful.

The second example deals with classroom/behavior management. It, too, deviates dramatically from the typical way textbooks discuss behavior management.

African American students are especially prone to have difficulty in school because of incompatibilities between the way many of them are encouraged to behave in their communities and the expectations of their teachers. Many African American males, and females as well, express their emotions much more intensely than most European Americans. When European American teachers observe African American males behave aggressively and assertively, too many of them assume that the students are much angrier or upset than they actually are. Attributing a level of anger to African American students that would be correct for European American students who behaved in a similar way, the teachers can become uncomfortable, even anxious, and concerned about what they incorrectly anticipate will happen next. As a result, they intervene when no intervention is necessary. If teachers appreciated the cultural context of African American males seemingly aggressive behavior towards others and understood that African American students displaying such aggressive behavior are unlikely to come to blows, they would be less likely to feel the need to intervene. This would lessen the likelihood that African American males would get into trouble needlessly and be referred to special education programs for students with behavior disorders.

Unfortunately, it is not possible for professors to select textbooks for their courses that pay more than lip service to diversity. Although there are a couple of textbooks that can be used in courses that focus primarily on diversity issues in special education, almost none of the current textbooks that are designed for courses on instructional methods, curriculum, assessment, counseling, classroom management, and so on discuss how special educators can adapt the techniques they include to the diverse group of students that are served by special education programs. I know of no research that explains why textbooks writers and publishers do not produce books that deal adequately with diversity. However, it may well be that they believe that nonbiased education textbooks would be unprofitable because the European American professors who teach the courses at which they are aimed would not order them.

As I write this book, I have three books in print dealing with diversity issues in special education. None of them are selling at anywhere near the rate their publishers or I expected. My editors and I have spoken at length about the possible causes of their lackluster sales. The conclusion we reached is that the causes are twofold. Special education professors are not very interested in the issues they raise. And they are not prepared to expend the time and effort necessary to learn the new material they contain and to include it in their courses.

About a year after the books became available I went to the annual Council for Exceptional Children's conference that was attended by many of the almost two thousand five hundred professors who had received desk copies of one or more of the books. Since I knew quite a few of these professors, I felt comfortable asking them what they thought of the books they had received. The professors of color and the few European American professors who were particularly interested in diversity issues made positive comments about the books. However, the comments of the European American professors to whom I spoke indicated that the majority of them hadn't even reviewed the books.

The following year, I attended the Council for Exceptional Children Symposium on Culturally and Linguistically Diverse Exceptional Learners. At this second conference, a great many professors told me how much they appreciated what I had written in my books and how useful the information that I had put at their disposal was in the courses they taught. I would like to say that my books had caught on from one year to the next. However, they had not. The explanation was otherwise. The professors at the conference who praised my work were almost all African Americans, Hispanic Americans, and Asian Pacific Island Americans. They were a biased sample of the professors in the field. Most of the presenters and attendees at the conference were people of color, since it was a conference on diversity.

The comments of four professors of color were especially enlightening. Three of them told me that at their universities faculty committees chose the textbooks for the courses they taught. And although each of them had recommended my books to the committees, the majority of the committee members (European American professors) had rejected their suggestions—sometimes rather adamantly. The fourth professor said that she had wanted to use one of my books in a course on diversity issues in special education, but the faculty would not approve adding the class to their list of courses.

These experiences helped to realize that I had crossed the line. In the 1970s 1980s and early 1990s, many European American professors found the multicultural content of my earlier books somewhat irrelevant. This time, I had included so much on diversity issues in my new books that my writing had become threatening or even offensive to many of them.

It appears that in todays' society, acceptance by people of color can be the kiss of death in the white world. It certainly seems to be the case with me.

Professors of special education must also use a variety of techniques such as lecturing, cooperative learning, small group discussion, and so on to meet needs of their students and to model what is required to meet the needs of elementary and secondary school students. They must allow students to select from a variety of assessment approaches the ones that enable them to demonstrate their competency. They should maintain flexible schedules for turning in papers and other work and completing course requirements. And so on.

Practicing what they should preach by using a variety of assessment, instructional, and classroom management approaches in their own classrooms, will be a real challenge to professors of special education. Many of them will have to change their attitudes about multicultural education, their belief that academic freedom bestows on professors the right to decide how to instruct and evaluate their students, and their concern that doing the right thing is not worth risking their relationships with colleagues or their tenure and promotion.

For 16 years I directed a bilingual/multicultural special education personnel preparation program. Many a time, students would angrily and resentfully complain to me that they felt that they were studying in two different programs. The faculty who taught the courses in the bilingual/ multicultural program were emphasizing how to adapt their methodology to the ethnic, socioeconomic class, contextual, and linguistic differences among students. However, diversity was seldom mentioned in their regular special education courses in which they were being taught that one method fits all students.

The last time I attended a conference of the Council for Exceptional Children, I made it a point to attend as many sessions that dealt with diversity as possible. What I saw was consistent and unfortunate: African American, Asian American, and Hispanic American professors presenting to other African American, Asian American, and Hispanic American professors and teachers. The situation had not changed very much since the 1960s. The people who had the greatest need to attend the sessions were elsewhere, participating in sessions that did not deal with diversity and which were not presented by non-European American professors.

For many years I was afraid that there might be something the matter with me that made me so critical of most of my colleagues. Why didn't I fit in at any of the universities I had worked in, I asked myself. Why didn't I attend the faculty social affairs? Why was I so angry with my colleagues? Why did they seem so self-centered and hypocritical? Who was I to put myself on a pedestal? Then I read a book about professors from working-class backgrounds that included the first person descriptions of twenty-some-odd working-class professors' university experiences. With very few exceptions, their experiences were like mine. They, too, felt alienated and separated from their middle-class colleagues. While many professors from working-class backgrounds described themselves as feeling guilty about leaving so many other working-class people behind and having a mission to improve the lot of working-class students, they found that their colleagues did not identify with their working-class students, and were not realistic about their needs. Like me, they also believed that their colleagues were more interested in their careers—in being granted tenure, earning promotions, and improving their status by publishing research and making presentations at conferences, than in their students' education and welfare.

The realization that my feelings and beliefs were shared by others, and that I was not alone, helped me to deal better with the class conflicts I experienced. But, it did not enable me to be more successful in my attempts to help my middle-class European American colleagues make their courses more relevant to working-class non-European American teachers in training and the working-class non-European American students with disabilities they would be teaching.

In the mid 1960s, the federal government funded a number of universities to develop personnel preparation programs for teachers of emotionally disturbed and behavior disordered students. To make sure we professors were not working separately to rediscover the wheel, the governments sponsored an annual two-day conference for us to share our ideas, knowledge, and experience. When, after a few years, budgets prevented the government from sponsoring our conference, we decided to piggyback our meeting with the annual conference of the Council for Exceptional Children, the major special education professional organization.

The meetings were great. They gave me an opportunity to share ideas and to learn what my colleagues were doing. They also provided us with a forum to provide the government with feedback about what we thought the government ought to do to assist us. Unfortunately, things changed. Some of my colleagues suggested that we organize ourselves into a formal group and become a division of the Council for Exceptional Children. I argued against it to no avail. The next annual meeting was devoted to forming subcommittees to write a constitution and by-laws and to do the other steps necessary to be incorporated into the organization. There were no discussions of the pressing problems that we should have been confronting, no open and honest discussions of controversial issues, no real communication. During the following annual meeting we discussed and approved all the paperwork that had been done; elected officers and representatives of our new parent organization; established a plethora of committees to plan our next annual meeting, to develop a newsletter, to plan a journal, and so on.

The whole atmosphere had changed. My colleagues were no longer interested in learning from each other. They were occupied with becoming officers and representatives, making presentations at the forthcoming conferences, and submitting articles for publication in the journal. In short, they were using the new organization to gain tenure and promotion at their "publish or perish" universities. They were more interested in their professional careers than their professional growth. Not long afterward, I discontinued my membership in the organization.

During the last conference of the organization that I attended, I was in a hotel lounge in Denver, Colorado talking to three other professors. We four were all that remained of a large group of professors who had been talking the night away about how schools and society dealt with behavior and emotionally disturbed kids. I realized that I felt a real affinity for them, and that they each had described how they had been fired, asked to leave, or denied tenure at least once while they were classroom teachers or professors.

That night I learned that professors who really wanted to help students should be prepared to experience the anger of their colleagues and administration and to pay the price for bucking the system. Most, but not all, of the professors that I have known who were ready to pay the price were non-European Americans. The three professors I just discussed however, were all committed middle-class European American males.

Each semester I ask the students in the courses on diversity issues in special education what they would need in order to do a good job with a group of diverse students. Invariably, their lists include detailed information about their students' cultures and the context of their lives, knowledge about how to adapt their educational techniques to the cultural and contextual needs of their students, the motivation to work hard and long, and the strength to make changes that would probably be unpopular with their administrations and communities.

Professors need these things as well in order to adapt what they teach and how they teach it to the needs of our diverse students. Unfortunately, most professors lack the information and the motivation to do the job. My guess is that many of them probably would also lack the courage to use the information if they had it. As a result, professors are not providing teachers in training with the information and skills they require to enable all students to succeed in our schools. And, they certainly are not modeling the kind of teaching that is necessary to meet the needs of the diverse group of students in America's schools and to bring about educational equality. Thus, until professors of special education become more representative of the students in the schools, and European American professors commit themselves to preparing teachers to succeed with all students in our schools, the current level of teacher unpreparedness will probably continue or worsen.

Special education personnel preparation programs should offer multicultural preparation. Most special educators do not know anything about how their poor and non-European American students live. To correct this, teacher training programs have to provide future teachers with first hand experience with poor and non-European American students (36). As Ewing points out:

> Improving school outcomes for African American children requires taking brave, bold, unusual steps...Until there is a wholehearted acceptance of the idea that major changes must occur in teacher education to improve schools for African American children, there is little promise for ameliorating the intensifying debacle currently facing the nation...teacher education programs must excel in preparing teachers and administrators who have an elevated level of authentic knowledge of African American culture; a deeper understanding of the impact African American culture has on behavior, learning styles, and preferred teaching styles; and a genuine appreciation for the valuable repertoire of experiences African American children bring to school...

preservice students must be immersed in extended, direct, real-life experiences in the African American milieu. Useful resources for gaining experiences, knowledge, and appreciation for African American cultural treasures systematically neglected in our schools include summer community-based programs; after school community-based student and parent learning centers; student teaching experiences; Big Brother-Big Sister programs; Urban League and NAACP community programs; and church-affiliated elder care, preschool day care, and after-school child care programs. (37 p.198-199)

In an ideal world, Ewing's recommendations would be followed by personnel preparation programs that prepare teachers to work with students from other ethnic backgrounds and students who are immigrants, migrants, homeless, and so on. However, in the less than ideal world in which we live, it would be impossible to provide teachers with the experiences they need to work effectively with all the different groups of diverse students in our schools. At the very least however, teacher preparation programs should target a few of the groups that are represented in their service areas and provide their students with intensive experience with these groups. Equally important, teacher preparation programs must teach educators the truth about prejudice and how to combat it. Until we eliminate the prejudice that infects our society, we will not be able to eliminate the prejudice in our school system that contributes so mightily to educational inequality. This will require identifying the specific courses in which these topics should be studied and monitoring to make sure that they are.

Finally, programs should prepare educators to be change agents rather than fit-in's because the status quo in schools is unacceptable. Students, especially those that are the victims of prejudice, must also be taught how to resist and combat it. This goal will not be very popular among professors. Most professors would agree that teachers' expectations for students, evaluation procedures, instructional techniques, curriculum materials, and classroom management techniques should be as free from bias as possible. However, they are unlikely to buck the system by modeling unbiased practices in their own classrooms. Professors learn early in their careers that fitting in is the way to survive and get ahead at most institutions of higher education. Professors who have learned this lesson and who possess personalities necessary to put it into practice will have difficulty preaching the opposite to their students.

REFERENCES

These references indicate that special educators are not and will continue not to be representative of the diverse group of students they serve.

1. American Association of Colleges for Teacher Education. (1994). *Teacher Education Pipeline III: Schools, Colleges, and Department of Education Enrollments by Race, Ethnicity, and Gender.* Washington, DC: Author.
2. Cook, L. H., & Boe, E. E. (1995). Who is teaching students with disabilities? *Teaching Exceptional Children,* 28(1), 70-72.
3. National Clearinghouse for Professionals in Special Education (1996). *A Summary of DPP Funding for Fiscal Year 1995.* Reston Va: Council for Exceptional Children.
4. Wald, J. (1996). *Culturally and Linguistically Diverse Populations in Special Education: A Demographic Analysis.* Reston, VA: Council for Exceptional Children.
5. U. S. Department of Education, Office of Special Education Programs. (1994). *Seventeenth Annual Report to Congress on the Implementation of the Individuals with Disabilities Education Act.* Washington, DC: Author.

The following references discuss the pro's and con's of adapting educational techniques to students' individual needs and reasons why some special educators and psychologists do so and others do not.

6. Grossman, H. (1995). *Educating Hispanic Students: Implications for Instruction, classroom Management, Counseling, and Assessment.* 2nd Ed. Springfield, IL: Thomas.
7. Grossman H. (1995). *Special Education in a Diverse Society.* Boston: Allyn & Bacon. p. 16
8. Suzuki, B. H. (1984). Curriculum transformation for multicultural education. *Education and Urban Society,* 16, 294-322.
9. Thomas, M. D. (1981). *Pluralism Gone Mad.* Bloomington, IN: Phi Delta Kappa Educational Foundation.
10. Nieto, S. (1992). *Affirming Diversity: The Sociopolitical Context of Multicultural Education.* New York: Longman.
11. Alley, J. (1980). Better understanding of the Indochinese students. *Education,* 101, 111-114.
12. Bernal, E. (1974). In a dialogue on cultural implications for learning. *Exceptional Children,* 40, 552-563.
13. Buriel, R. (1984). Integration with traditional Mexican-American culture and sociocultural adjustment. In J. L. Martinez Jr. & Mendoza, R. H. *Chicano Psychology* 2nd Ed. Orlando, FL: Academic Press.
14. Buriel, R., & Saenz, E. (1980). Psychocultural characteristics of college bound and non-college bound Chicanos. *Journal of Social Psychology,* 110, 245-251.
15. Cloud, N. (1991). Acculturation of Ethnic Minorities. In A. M. Ambert (Ed.), *Bilingual Education and English as a Second Language: A Research Handbook* 1988-

1990. New York: Garland.

16. Ellis, A. A. (1980). *The Assimilation and Acculturation of Indochinese Children into American Culture.* ERIC ED 213 484.

17. ERIC/CUE. (1985). The social and psychological adjustment of Southeast Asian Refugees. *Urban Review,* 17(2), 147-152.

18. Higham, J. (1984). *Send These to Me: Immigrants in Urban America.* Baltimore, MD: Johns Hopkins University Press.

19. Hilliard, A. G. III (1992). *Language, Culture, and Valid Teaching.* Paper presented at the Topical Conference on Cultural and Linguistically Diverse Exceptional Children. Minneapolis.

20. Irvine, J. J. (1991). *Black Students and School Failure: Policies, Practices, and Prescriptions.* New York: Praeger.

21. Landsman, M., Padilla, A., Clark, C., Liederman, H., Ritter, P., & Dornbusch, S. (1990). *Biculturality and Academic Achievement among Asian and Hispanic Adolescents.* Paper presented at the annual meeting of the National Association for Bilingual Education, Tucson.

22. Longstreet, W. S. (1978). *Aspects of Ethnicity.* New York: Teachers College Press.

23. Melville, M. B. (1980). Selective acculturation of female Mexican migrants. In M. B. Melville (Ed.), *Twice a Minority: Mexican American Women.* St. Louis: Mosby.

24. Morales, R. F. (Ed.). (1983). *Bridging Cultures.* Los Angeles: Asian American Health Training Center.

25. Niera, C. (1988). Building 860. *Harvard Educational Review,* 58(2), 337-342.

26. Patrick, J. L. (1986). Immigration in the Curriculum. *Social Education,* 50(3), 172-176.

27. Santiseban, D., & Szapocznik, J. (1982). Substance abuse disorders among Hispanics: A focus on prevention. In R. M. Becerra, M. Karno, & J. I. Escobar (Eds.), *Mental Health and Hispanics: Clinical Perspectives.* New York: Grune & Stratton.

28. So, A. Y. (1987). High-achieving disadvantages students: A study of low SES Hispanic language minority students. *Urban Education,* 22(1), 19-35.

29. Szapocznik, J., Kurtines, W. M., & Fernandez, T. (1979). *Bicultural Involvement and Adjustment in Hispanic Youths.* ERIC ED 193 374.

30. Torres-Matrullo, C. M. (1980). Acculturation, sex-role values and mental health among mainland Puerto Ricans. In A. M. Padilla (Ed.), *Acculturation: Theory, Models, and Some New Findings.* Boulder, CO: Westview Press.

31. Vigil, J. D. (1982). Chicano high schoolers: Educational performance and acculturation. *Educational Forum,* 47(1), 58-73.

32. Wei, T. T. D. (1980). *Vietnamese Refugee Students: A Handbook for School Personnel.* ERIC ED 208 109.

This reference indicates that the vast majority of teacher trainers are European American.

33. Zimpher, N., & Ashburn, E. (1992). Countering parochialism in teacher candi dates. In M. Dilworth (Ed.), *Diversity in Teacher Education*. San Francisco: Jossey-Bass.

Information about the factors that influence educators' decisions about whether to enroll in doctorate programs is found in these publications.

34. Boone, R. S., & Ruhl, K. L. (1995). Controllable factors in recruitment of minority and nonminority individuals for doctoral study in special education. In B. A. Ford (Ed.), *Multiple Voices for Ethnically Diverse Exceptional Learners*. Reston, VA: Council for Exceptional Children.
35. Wright, D. J. (1987). Minority students: Developmental beginnings. In D. J. Wright (Ed.), *Responding to the Needs of Today's Minority Students*. San Francisco: Jossey-Bass.

Evidence of the positive effects of practical teaching experience with ethnically different exceptional students is found in the following reference.

36. Minner, S. & Prater G. (1994). *Preparing Special Educators for Work in Rural Areas. Two Field-Based Programs That Work*. ERIC ED369 612.

The quote about providing special educators with meaningful life experiences with African American exceptional students is found in this publication.

37. Ewing, N. J. (1994). Restructured teacher education for inclusiveness: A dream deferred for African American children. In B. A. Ford, F. E. Obiakor,& J. E. Patton. *Effective Education of African American Exceptional Learners*. Austin, TX: Pro-ed. p. 198-199.

Chapter 5

CONCLUDING COMMENTS

All special educators can and should contribute to making the special education system more equitable for poor, non European American, immigrant, refugee, migrant, rural, and limited English proficient students with disabilities. Because middle-class European American professionals comprise the preponderance of those who staff special education programs, they can do the most to correct it. A few of them are doing all in their power to do so; the vast majority are not. The question is whether these others will have the strength to face their shortcomings, especially their prejudice and ignorance, the humanity required to adapt the special education system to the needs of students who are least like them, and the commitment required to devote the additional time and effort that these adaptations necessitate.

Special educators of color who understand from experience the neglect and discriminatory treatment described in this book, have a pivotal role to play in the improvement of our special education system. They are in the best positions to inform and educate their European American colleagues about its true nature and to model the behavior necessary to correct it. For special educators of color to do so takes a great deal of courage because in our prejudiced society, they risk alienating their colleagues with whom they have to work and on whom they have to depend for tenure, promotions, and the like. Despite these risks, many of them are doing all they can to change things. Others however, need to increase their efforts. The question is whether they will dare to do so.

I learned an important lesson about the pace of change while living in Tuskegee, Alabama in the late 1960s and early 1970s. Until the late 1960s, Tuskegee was a segregated southern town like hundreds of other small cities in the South. By the time I arrived in Tuskegee in 1969, many changes had occurred. African Americans had the right to vote. The county had an African American sheriff (played by Jim Brown in a Hollywood movie) and a number of African American deputy sheriffs. Schools were integrated. Well, not really. The local whites had left the public school system, but they had left the European American superintendent in charge of the schools they had fled. And, they had stripped the buildings of equipment that they had put to good use in their private school system.

The local movie house was integrated. Actually, the African Americans refused to sit in the balcony so the European American owner closed down the theater. The town pool was integrated. Well, not really. The African Americans had insisted on swimming in the pool. The town fathers had built the African Americans their own swimming pool. The African Americans had swum in both, so the whites built themselves a private one. The local restaurants were integrated. Actually, the European American-owned establishment that had tables and chairs either closed down or turned into take-out places. African Americans had been given jobs in the local banks and shops but only after a boycott and only as tellers and clerks. Hardly any African Americans were running cash registers in European American-owned stores. African Americans were able to use public toilets in the local gas stations. However, that had not happened until a young black male had been shot to death while trying to use a "for-whites-only" toilet, and the person who shot him had been exonerated by an all European American jury of his peers. In 1969, to an outside observer it appeared that considerable progress had occurred since separate but equal had been declared unconstitutional.

By the time I left Tuskegee in 1973, the superintendent of schools had "resigned." An African American had bought and reopened the movie theater. An African American had built and was operating the first African American-owned supermarket in town. An enterprising European American had opened a new restaurant with tables and chairs that served African Americans and any European Americans who cared or dared to eat there. The African American majority in Tuskegee had even elected their first black mayor. To an outside observer it appeared that considerable progress had occurred between 1969 and 1973.

Not really. When I spoke to the old-timers in town or to the professors on campus many of them spoke proudly of the progress they had achieved in the 1950s and 1960s, the battles they had won, and the price they and others had paid. The high school kids and young college students however, saw it different-ly. They had not lived a lifetime under segregation. They hadn't had to lower their eyes when a European American woman was walking in their direction. They hadn't been told that "nigras can't float so ya'll don't need no pool." They hadn't had to sit in "nigger heaven" at the movie theater. They hadn't attended some raggedy school with hand-me-down textbooks that the white folks had no more use for. So they didn't experience the same progress. They focused on the many things that were still unfair. They complained that the politicians in Montgomery (the capital of Alabama) were spending their tax money on white colleges and very little on black schools, that they were giving lots of state scholarships to students at white schools but not to Tuskegee stu-dents, and that they were building a white state-supported college right next to a black one that offered the same programs so that the whites would have their own school. They complained that it was time that the highway patrol stop being a cracker-run and staffed organization that harassed the hell out of black folks, that it was time for blacks to get more responsible, higher paying jobs in the white-owned establishments in town, time for the state to start hiring black-owned construction companies, and so on.

They were talking about restarting the boycotts of the 1960s. And they probably were just as angry about the injustices they experienced as their parents and their parents' parents had been about the injustices they had had to suffer.

I guess if I go back to Tuskegee next year I will see that the twenty-some-odd years since 1973 have seen even more "progress." But I'll bet the current group of high school and college students will be complaining just as much as the students complained while I was there. And, they will probably be just as angry about the injustices they are experiencing. Perhaps they will be angry enough to organize a new round of boycotts and demonstrations and I won't blame them.

I do not want to add my voice to those calling for tokenism and half-hearted changes that do not benefit students sufficiently. Halfway solutions are insufficient solutions. While none of us can contribute more than partially to the solution of the inequality in special education, we all must aim for a complete solution. That is the only way we will accomplish the whole task. If we all do our part, we can move mountains.

It's easy for special educators to say that change is an evolutionary process that proceeds slowly, or to claim that inequality always has been and always will be with us because we cannot change human nature. However, special educators do not have the right to adopt such an attitude. People who are not suffering injustice should not be pointing to the progress that the previous generation made and telling today's students with disabilities and their parents to be patient. Why should they be patient? They are suffering injustice. What right do people have to ask them to settle for a half a loaf even for a little while, if they are not suffering the same injustices and are eating from a full loaf?

As I said, I learned a lesson from my experience in Tuskegee. Slow and steady progress is not good enough. The elimination of inequalities in special education has to be not only rapid and continuous, but as immediate and complete as possible.